P9-CBS-645

GOOD
HOUSEKEEPING
1, 2, 3 Cook!

YUM!
Ooey-Gooey
Cinnamon
Rolls!

GOOD HOUSEKEEPING

1, 2, 3 Cook!

My First Cookbook

Foreword by Kate Merker

What do you call a small portion of macaroni with cheese?
Snac-N-Cheese
Dad Jokes Mac and Cheese page 60

CONTENTS

Get ready to have some cooking fun in 1, 2, 3!

Why You'll Love This Book

From the time I was very young, I remember sitting at countless kitchen tables where the food was being prepared–measuring, mixing, smelling and always tasting the recipe along the way.

The cooks in charge were my grandparents, parents and friends, each with different ideas of what to make and how to make food taste good. After a while I noticed that even if we started with the same list of ingredients, what we made in one kitchen could be completely different in another. And everyone shared their secrets.

A pinch of something with my fingers was totally different from my father's pinch or my grandmother's and is now completely different when my children and their friends are my helpers. That is the beauty of food and cooking with others—it varies depending on who participates.

There was one thing that existed in every kitchen, though, and that was the joy that comes from working together to cook food with and for people you love. Whether it is baked or sautéed, boiled or broiled, every dish celebrates that joy, and that is exactly what this book is all about: sharing with young chefs the pure pleasure of cooking.

Cooking is an adventure (make sure to taste everything along the way!). Every kitchen experience, no matter the outcome, is filled with invention, learning and sometimes even intrigue (How did that cake rise so high?). Your results will turn into your own kitchen memories and perhaps form the stories that you will share through generations. Trust the recipes here to be an excellent guide and just remember that your pinch decides the final and special outcome.

Enjoy!
Kate

- Chapter 1 -

Welcome to the Kitchen!

Hey, parents! Cooking with your child is a wonderful way to work together and have fun, all while developing kitchen know-how and practicing early math and literacy skills. Many of the recipes in this book involve working with heat, knives, blenders, or other kitchen tools. We've marked these steps with this helping hands symbol. You know your child best, so use your judgment in gauging what your child is ready to do on their own and when they'll need your help.

What do you call baby potatoes?

Tater tots.

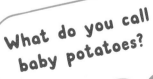

Meet the Team!

The first issue of *Good Housekeeping* was published in 1885. That means *Good Housekeeping* editors have been testing products (including toys!) for more than 135 years. The editors and cooks in the Test Kitchen create tasty recipes, making them over and over again until they are just right. The recipes in this cookbook were all made by a team of chefs who love cooking—just like you! Let's find out more about why they like to be in the kitchen.

What was your favorite food when you were a kid?

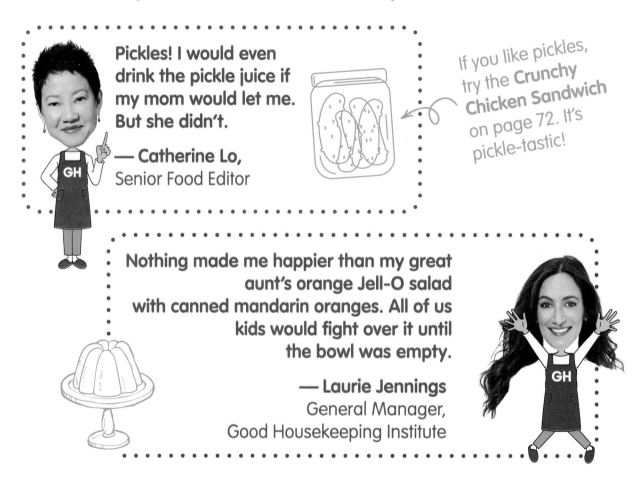

Pickles! I would even drink the pickle juice if my mom would let me. But she didn't.

— Catherine Lo,
Senior Food Editor

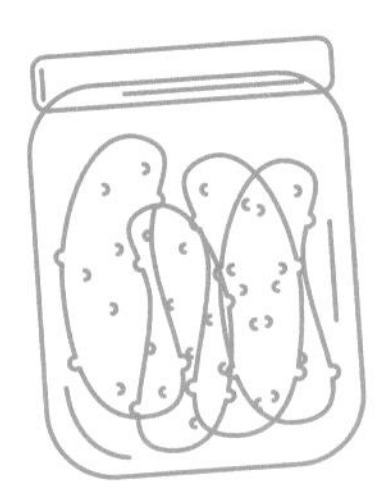

If you like pickles, try the **Crunchy Chicken Sandwich** on page 72. It's pickle-tastic!

Nothing made me happier than my great aunt's orange Jell-O salad with canned mandarin oranges. All of us kids would fight over it until the bowl was empty.

— Laurie Jennings
General Manager,
Good Housekeeping Institute

What was the first thing you learned to cook?

Scrambled eggs! I was a picky eater, so my dad taught me his recipe so that I could feed myself something nutritious that I loved.

—Becca Miller,
Associate Food Editor

Do you love scrambled eggs, too? Then try **Egg-stremely Cheesy Sammies** on page 28.

Lasagna! I used to help my mom make it for dinner, and while she wasn't looking I would eat the cooked noodles and we'd have to make more!

—Stefani Sassos
Deputy Director, Nutrition Lab

Who taught you how to cook?

My family: parents, grandparents, aunts and uncles. Everyone was in the kitchen and everyone had a job.

—Kate Merker,
Chief Food Director

What's your favorite thing to cook?

My favorite thing to make is fresh pasta. I have a wooden *chitarra* that kind of looks like a guitar that I use to hand-roll spaghetti alla chitarra.

—Eva Bleyer,
Home & Kitchen Appliance Reviews Analyst

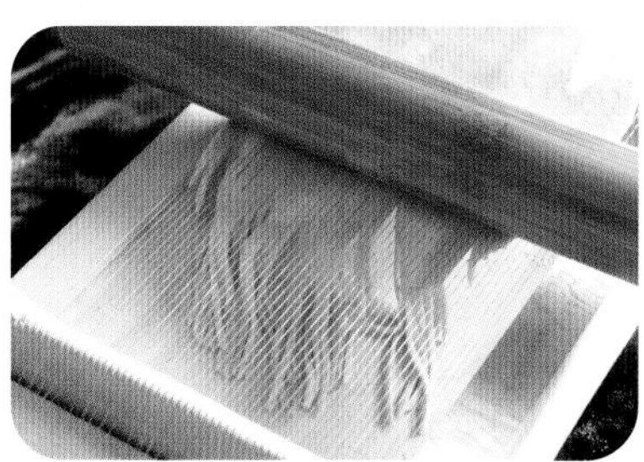

To make spaghetti with a *chitarra*, pasta dough is rolled over the strings, which then cut the dough into long, rectangular spaghetti strands.

What food did you hate as a kid but you love now?

Bananas. I used to tell my mom "no nana" when I was a baby, but learned to love them as the sweet, creamy, dessert-like fruit they are.

—Samantha MacAvoy,
Editorial Assistant

What was the first vegetable you loved, but didn't think you would?

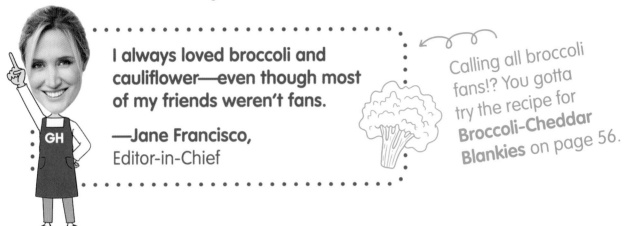

I always loved broccoli and cauliflower—even though most of my friends weren't fans.

—Jane Francisco,
Editor-in-Chief

Calling all broccoli fans!? You gotta try the recipe for **Broccoli-Cheddar Blankies** on page 56.

Who is your favorite person to cook with?

I love cooking with my friend, Alyssa. She's a private chef and we love trying new ingredients and techniques together.

—Nicole Papantoniou,
Deputy Director, Kitchen Appliances & Technology Lab

Start Cooking in 1, 2, 3!

Have you ever been curious about how ingredients can be mixed together and then cooked or baked to make a delicious dinner or sweet and tasty treat? Follow these steps on your cooking adventure:

1. Check in with your tummy—what sounds yummy?
2. Pick a recipe—maybe breakfast or lunch or something sweet to munch! ✋ THIS means a step might be a little tricky to do on your own, so make sure a grown-up is there to help you out.
3. Set down the book and get ready to cook!

Get Ready to Cook!

Before you get to crackin' any eggs, here are some tips to make your time in the kitchen a piece of cake . . . or should we say MUG of cake?

Hold up *What's a mug of cake?* Find out and learn how to make one yourself on page 114.

1. **Clean!** Sing the *ABC* song as you wash your hands in warm, soapy water. After *Z*, dry your hands really well with a clean towel—make sure they aren't wet and slippery!

2. **Plan!** Read the recipe from start to finish and check the fridge, cupboards, and pantry to make sure you have everything you'll need. It's a bummer to find out you're missing an ingredient after you've already started cooking!

3. **Prepare!** Before you start, wash any fruits and veggies you might need and measure out your ingredients ahead of time. Now you're ready to cook!

Get to Know Your Kitchen Tools

dry measuring cups

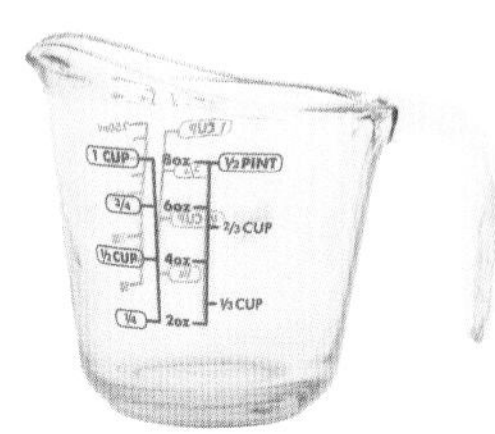

liquid measuring cup

measuring spoons

mixing bowl

Tip Keep your bowl from tipping while mixing with this cool trick: Twirl a dish towel into a snake, connect the ends with a chip clip or binder clip and rest the bowl right on top.

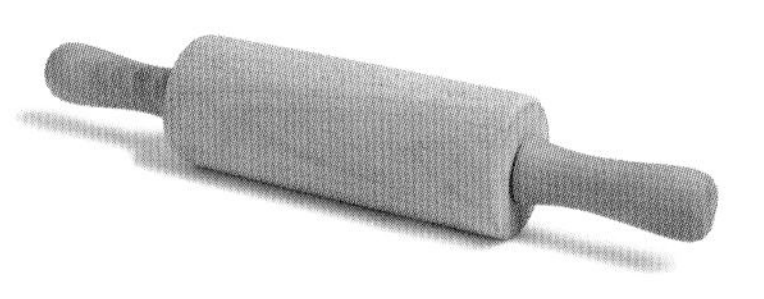

rolling pin

silicone spatula

baking sheet

Tip Dip cookie cutters in flour first to keep them from sticking to the dough. (Adults: Wash and dry cutters by hand so nonstick coatings on them don't wear off in the dishwasher.)

cookie cutters

Here's a hint! Flip the zester over and pull the tool over the citrus so you can see the zester in action.

colander/strainer

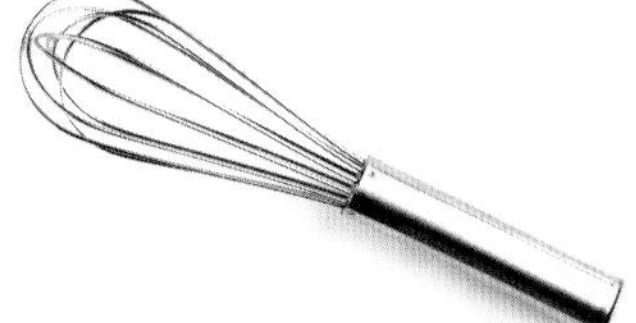

whisk

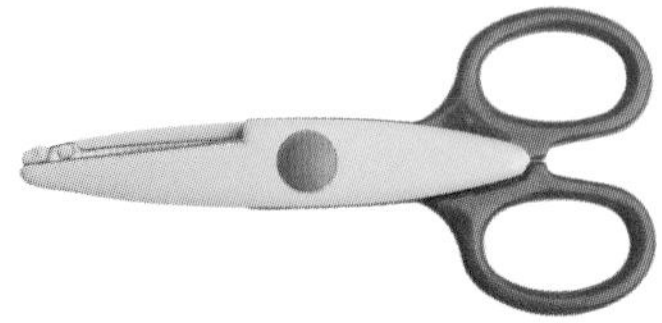

kids' safety scissors

Tip When cutting, keep your fingers away from the blade. Use one to hand to move the knife across the food, while using your other hand to keep the food still.

kids' safety knife

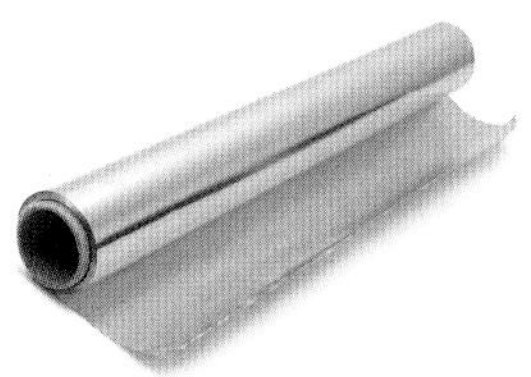

aluminum foil

parchment paper

One of the best ways to become a great cook is to taste as you go! Keep a bunch of teaspoons on hand while cooking to taste and season your dish.

Kitchen Basics in 1, 2, 3

Measuring Liquids

1. Gather your equipment! You will need a glass measuring cup and the liquid you are measuring.

2. Place the measuring cup on a level, flat surface. Pour the liquid into the measuring cup and wait for it to stop moving.

Try your hand at measuring liquids when you make the **Chocolate Caramel Mug Cake** on page 114.

3. Bend down until your eyes are at the same level as the side of the measuring cup and look to make sure the liquid is even with the measurement line.

Measuring Dry Ingredients (like Flour or Sugar)

1. Gather your equipment! You will need measuring cups with handles, the ingredient you are measuring, and a butter knife.

2. Use a spoon to scoop up the ingredient and add it to the measuring cup. Using a spoon is one way to avoid adding too much of an ingredient to your recipe. Fill the measuring cup until the ingredient is slightly above the edge of the cup.

3. Gently tap the top of the measuring cup with a butter knife to evenly distribute the ingredient inside the cup. Then drag the flat edge of the knife across the top of the cup to knock off any extra ingredient.

Practice measuring when you make **Cocoa Cool Cookie Sandwiches** on page 106!

Cracking Eggs

1. Gather your equipment! You will need the eggs called for in the recipe and a bowl.

2. Crack the egg on a flat, clean surface.

3. Use both hands to hold the egg over the bowl and gently pull the egg shells apart at the break. The egg will plop into the bowl. Repeat with other eggs if necessary.

Try this by making the **Egg-stremely Cheesy Sammies** on page 28.

Tip If egg shells fall into the bowl, don't worry. Use one half of the shell to scoop them out or use your fingertip.

Juicing Citrus

1. Gather your equipment! You will need the citrus fruit called for in the recipe, a knife and cutting board, a bowl and a fork.

2. Roll the lemon, lime, or orange on a flat, clean surface to soften the fruit and loosen its juice. Plus, it will smell good! ✋ Then have an adult help and cut the fruit in half.

3. Hold one of the halves over the bowl and squeeze out the juice, turning and squeezing the half a couple of times. Then squeeze the second half. Use a fork to remove any seeds that may have fallen into the bowl.

Juice an orange for the **Best-Ever Flank Steak** marinade on page 74.

Lining Baking Sheets

1. Gather your equipment! You will need a rimmed baking sheet or cookie sheet and parchment paper.

2. Pull a length of parchment paper across the pan to measure how much you'll need.

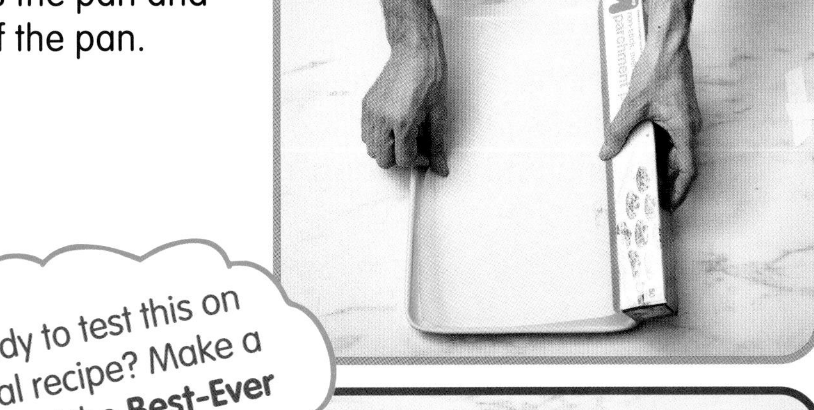

3. Cut the parchment paper to the same size as the pan and place it on top of the pan.

Ready to test this on a real recipe? Make a batch of the **Best-Ever Granola** on page 40.

Greasing Pans

1. Gather your equipment! You will need a jug of oil, tablespoon, small bowl, paper towel, and pan.

2. Pour a tablespoon or two of oil into the bowl and dip in the paper towel.

3. Rub the pan with the paper towel, making sure to get all the corners and edges. Dip the paper towel in the oil once more if needed.

This will come in handy when you make the **Really Lucky Shamrock Cupcakes** on page 130.

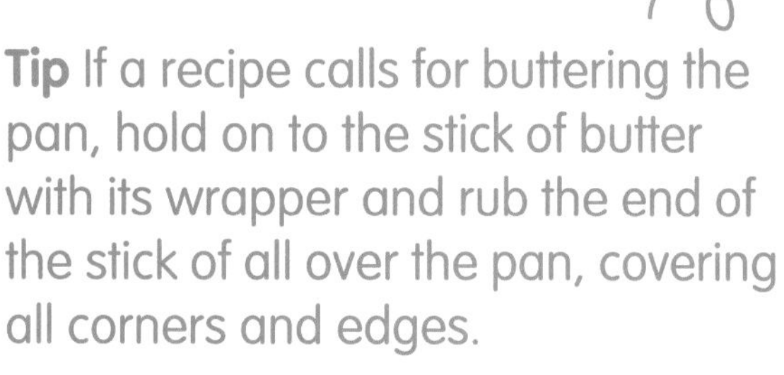

Tip If a recipe calls for buttering the pan, hold on to the stick of butter with its wrapper and rub the end of the stick of all over the pan, covering all corners and edges.

Rolling Dough

1. Gather your equipment! You will need parchment paper, dough, and a rolling pin. If you have them, silicone rolling pin rings make it easy to measure the thickness of the dough!

2. Spread one sheet of parchment paper on your work surface and place the dough in the center. Cover with a second sheet of parchment paper and begin rolling, starting in the center of the dough and rolling to the edge.

3. Turn the circle of dough an inch or two to the right and roll out again to make it even. Check to make sure the dough is an even thickness throughout.

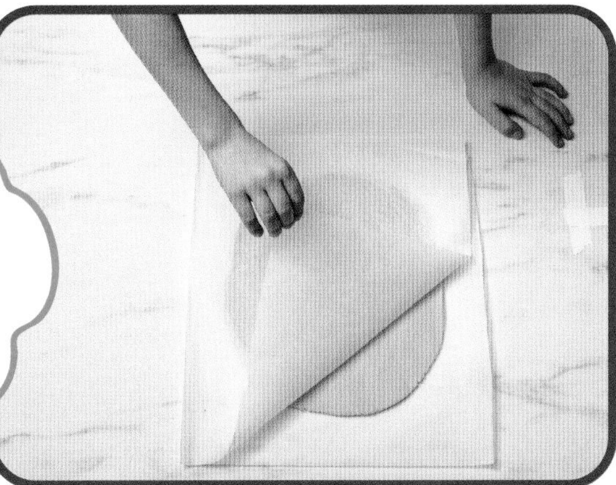

Roll out dough for real when you make the **Ooey-Gooey Cinnamon Rolls** on page 42.

Spreading, Sauce on a Pizza

1. Gather your equipment! You will need a spoon, sauce, and dough that's already shaped out on a baking sheet. If you need help shaping out dough, see page 66!

2. Scoop up a spoonful of sauce and place it in the center of the dough.

3. Use the back of the spoon to spread the sauce over the dough, leaving an inch of space uncovered along the edges. Add more sauce if you like.

Test your sauce spreading skills by making **The Queen's Pizza** on page 66.

Spreading Frosting on Cookies

1. Gather your equipment! You will need prepared cookies, frosting, and an offset spatula.
2. Scoop up a bit of frosting with the offset spatula.

3. Spread the frosting onto the cookie, leaving the edges unfrosted so you have a place to grab your cookie.

Tip An offset spatula is kitchen tool with a long, narrow dull blade that helps you spread frosting in a smooth, even layer. Its handle is angled to keep your hands out of the way.

Follow these directions when you make the **Here Comes Peter Cottontail Cookies** on page 144.

page 28
page 32
page 34
YUM YUM
page 36
page 40
page 42
yum
page 46
page 48
page 51
YUM YUM

- Chapter 2 -

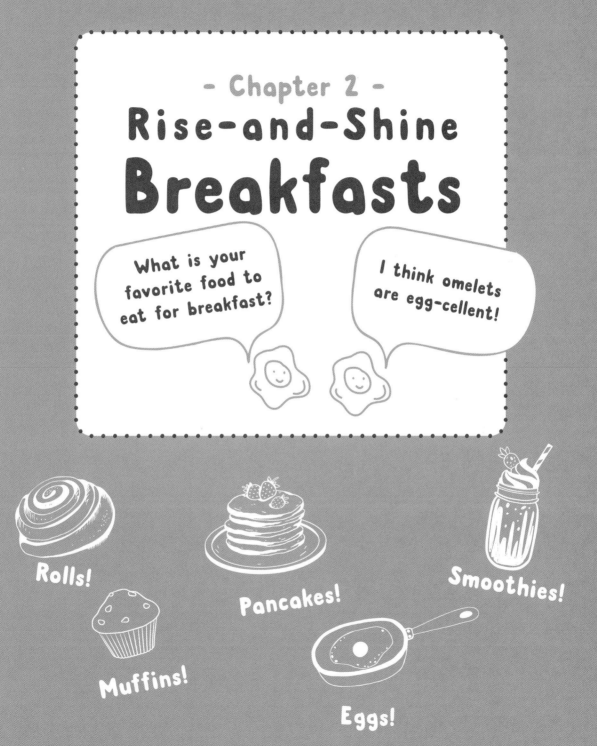

Rise-and-Shine Breakfasts

What is your favorite food to eat for breakfast?

I think omelets are egg-cellent!

Rolls!

Muffins!

Pancakes!

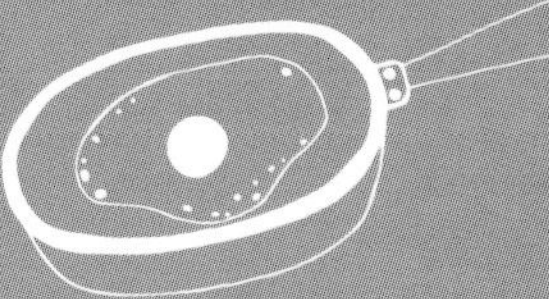

Eggs!

Smoothies!

Egg-stremely Cheesy Sammies

Prepare Your Ingredients

4 English muffins

4 large eggs

1 tablespoon water

Kosher salt and cracked pepper

1 tablespoon extra virgin olive oil

2 ounces extra-sharp Cheddar cheese, grated (about ½ cup)

1 cup baby spinach

4 thin slices ham (optional)

Serves 4

Ready to eat in 10 minutes

Gather Your Kitchen Tools

Fork

Toaster

4 plates

Medium bowl

Large nonstick skillet

Silicone spatula

Spoon

If bits of shell get into your bowl of cracked eggs, try scooping them out with a bigger piece of eggshell. Otherwise you can try using your finger. Either way, you might find that little bit of shell tries to run away!

Make Your Egg-stremely Cheesy Sammies

1. Using a fork, split the English muffins in half. Toast them and put them on plates so they're ready when the eggs are cooked.

2. Crack the eggs into a medium bowl by following the directions on page 19. Add the water, a pinch of salt and a pinch of pepper to the eggs. With the fork, beat the eggs until everything is mixed well.

To **beat** means to stir quickly until smooth using a whisk, spoon, fork or mixer.

3. Add the olive oil to a nonstick skillet on medium. Once the oil is hot, pour the egg mixture into the pan. As the eggs cook, gently stir them with a silicone spatula. After 2 to 3 minutes, the eggs will begin to clump together and become less runny. Cook them until they're as scrambled as you like.

4. Spoon some scrambled eggs onto the bottom half of each muffin. Sprinkle a little of the grated cheese on top, then add some spinach and a slice of ham if using. Top each sandwich with the other muffin half and enjoy!

To **grate** means to break food down into small, thin strips with a knife or a grater.

Egg-cellent Info

Eggs come in different sizes. Medium, large and extra-large are the most common. We test recipes with large eggs so be sure to use them for the recipes in this book.

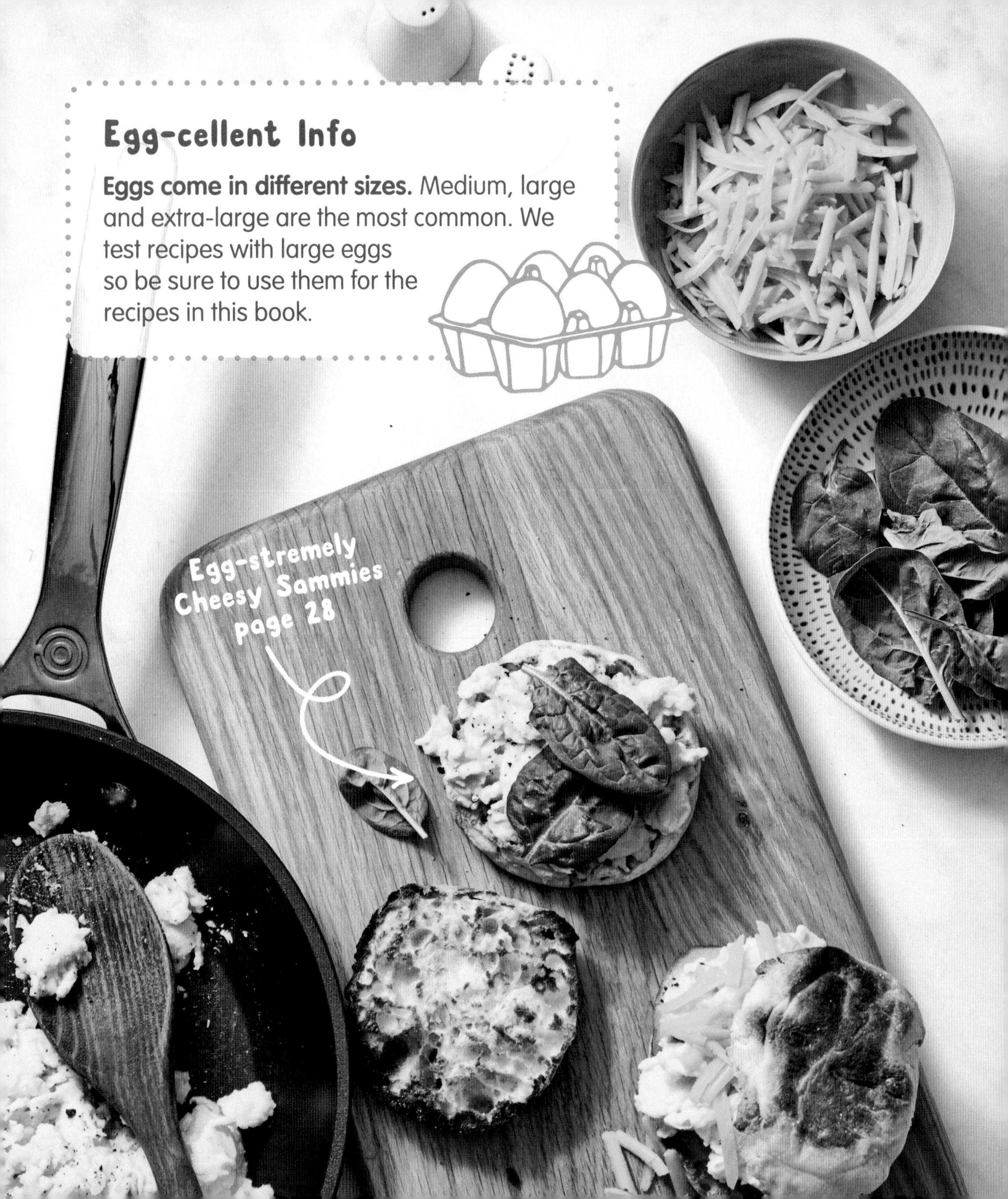

Hello, Frittata Muffins page 32
You will want to say "hello" instead of "ta-ta" to these frittata muffins!
"Ta-ta" is a way to say "goodbye."

Hello, Frittata Muffins

Prepare Your Ingredients

Nonstick cooking spray

6 large eggs

½ cup milk

Kosher salt and pepper

¾ cup crumbled soft goat cheese

5 ounces baby spinach, chopped

½ cup roasted red pepper, diced

2 ounces ham, sliced into ribbons

Serves 6

Ready to eat in 50 minutes

Gather Your Kitchen Tools

12-cup muffin pan

Large bowl

Whisk or fork

Measuring cups

Silicone spatula

Ladle

Oven mitts

Wire rack

Most ladles can scoop up ½ cup, so for this recipe, fill the ladle only halfway.

Make Your Hello, Frittata Muffins

1. Heat the oven to 350°F. Lightly coat the muffin pan with nonstick cooking spray.
2. Crack the eggs into a large bowl and then beat them with a whisk or fork. Add the milk, a pinch of salt and a pinch of pepper and beat to combine. Using a silicone spatula, stir in the cheese, spinach and diced roasted red pepper.

To **dice** means to cut food into very small cubes.

3. Using a ladle, carefully scoop the batter into the muffin cups. Try to fill each cup evenly, using about ¼ cup of batter per cup. Divide the ham evenly among the cups.
4. Bake until the muffins don't jiggle anymore, 20 to 25 minutes. Using oven mitts, remove the muffin pan from the oven. Let the muffins cool on a wire rack for 5 minutes, then remove them from the cups. Enjoy them while they're warm!

To **bake** means to cook food in an oven.

Get to Know Your Egg Dishes

A frittata is a lot like two other egg dishes—omelets and quiche. An omelet is cooked fast on the stovetop. A frittata is either cooked slow on the stovetop or baked. A quiche is also baked, but unlike a frittata, it has a crust. All three can be filled with meat and veggies and are very yummy.

Challah if You Love French Toast

Prepare Your Ingredients

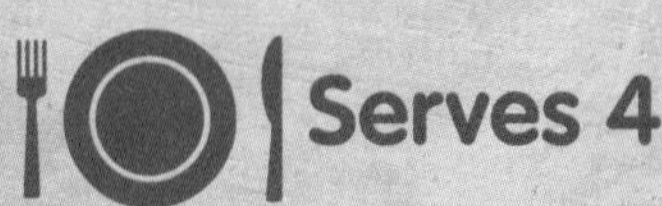

3 large eggs

¾ cup whole milk

¾ teaspoon ground cinnamon

¾ teaspoon pure vanilla extract

2 tablespoons unsalted butter, divided

4 1-inch-thick slices challah bread

Yogurt, berries and pure maple syrup or honey, for serving

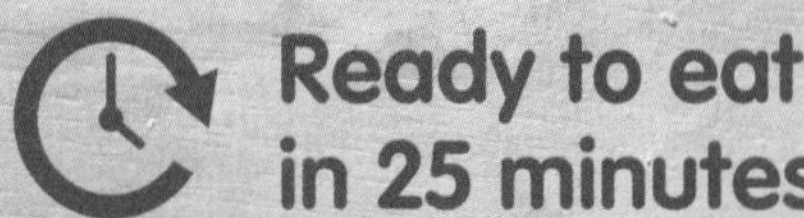

Gather Your Kitchen Tools

Large, shallow bowl

Measuring cups

Whisk or fork

Large nonstick skillet

Pancake turner

Wire rack

YUM Berries!!

What types of berries do you see?

Try raisin bread instead of challah, for a tasty twist!

Make Your French Toast

To **whisk** means to stir ingredients briskly together with a fork or whisk to mix, blend or add air.

1. Crack the eggs into a bowl by following the directions on page 19. Add the milk, cinnamon and vanilla to the eggs and whisk to combine.

2. Add ½ tablespoon butter to a skillet on medium-low. As the pan heats up and the butter melts, move on to the next step. (But keep an eye on the butter—if it starts to smoke, lower the heat.)

3. Place a bread slice into the egg mixture. Let the bread soak in the mixture for a minute. Using a fork, carefully flip it onto the other side and let it soak for another minute. (The bread should become a little soggy and might be tricky to flip. Practice makes perfect!)

4. Use your fingers to carefully place the egg-soaked bread slice into the hot pan. Cook for 2 minutes, then flip the bread over with the pancake turner. Cook the other side until golden brown, about 2 minutes more. Once the bread is browned and no longer soggy, remove it from the pan and place it on a wire rack to cool. (You can cook one slice at a time or multiple slices at once, if your pan is big enough.) Repeat with the remaining bread slices, adding more butter to the pan for each.

5. Serve with yogurt, berries, maple syrup or anything else you like!

Two pieces of bread were about to race. One piece looked at the other and said, "You're toast!"

Yum-O Yogurt Pancakes

Prepare Your Ingredients

1 cup all-purpose flour

¾ teaspoon baking soda

½ teaspoon baking powder

¼ teaspoon kosher salt

½ cup vanilla-flavored Greek yogurt

⅓ cup milk

2 large eggs

2 tablespoons pure maple syrup

1 teaspoon pure vanilla extract

1 tablespoon unsalted butter

Yogurt, strawberries, blueberries and syrup, for serving

Peek under the pancake with a pancake turner to make sure it is golden brown before you flip it.

Serves 4

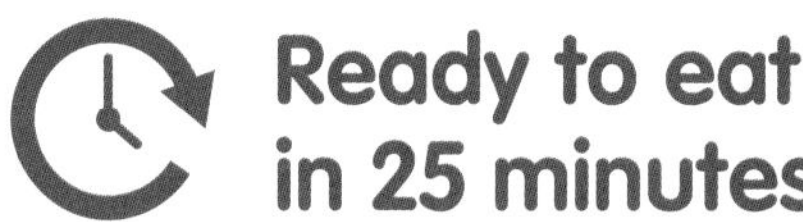

Ready to eat in 25 minutes

Gather Your Kitchen Tools

2 large bowls

Measuring cups and spoons

Whisk

Silicone spatula

Large nonstick skillet

Large spoon

Pancake turner

Wire rack

Aluminum foil

Make Your Yum-O Yogurt Pancakes

1. In a large bowl, whisk together the flour, baking soda, baking powder and salt, following the directions on page 18. Set aside.

2. In a separate large bowl, whisk together the yogurt, milk, eggs, maple syrup and vanilla. See page 19 for how to crack the eggs.

Fun Food Fact!
Greek yogurt has more water strained out of it than regular yogurt, which makes it much thicker.

3. Add the flour mixture to the yogurt mixture. Using a silicone spatula, stir to combine. (The batter will be thick, so mixing might be hard work!)

4. Heat a skillet on medium and add a tablespoon of butter. Check the heat by sprinkling the pan with water—when the water bubbles and evaporates immediately, the pan is hot enough.

5. Using a large spoon, scoop about 2 tablespoons of the batter and pour it onto the hot pan. Drop as many scoops as will fit on the pan, leaving and inch or two of space between each pancake. Watch the batter as it cooks; when bubbles begin to appear on the top, it's time to flip! Using a pancake turner, carefully flip each pancake over, then cook until the underside is golden brown, about another minute. Transfer the cooked pancakes to a wire rack. Cover the pancakes loosely with foil to keep them warm.

TIP Are your pancakes sticking? Add 1 teaspoon of oil and heat it before cooking the next batch.

6. When you're ready to eat, enjoy the pancakes topped with yogurt, strawberries, blueberries and syrup.

Pancake Shapes

A fun thing to do with pancakes when they are cooked is to cut out shapes with cookie cutters. Be creative!

More Granola, Please!

Make your own mix! Start with the main recipe and just make a few swaps. Try these:

Let the granola cool and toss with ¼ cup mini chocolate chips

Replace pumpkin seeds with 1½ cups raw almonds. When cool, toss with ⅓ cup dried apricots, chopped.

Let cool and toss with ¼ cup craisins and ¼ cup dried blueberries.

Best-Ever Granola page 40

Best-Ever Granola

Prepare Your Ingredients

½ cup extra virgin olive oil or extra virgin coconut oil, melted

¾ cup pure maple syrup

1 teaspoon kosher salt

3 cups old-fashioned rolled oats

1 cup unsweetened coconut flakes

¾ cup raw sunflower seeds

¾ cup raw pumpkin seeds

Makes 7 cups

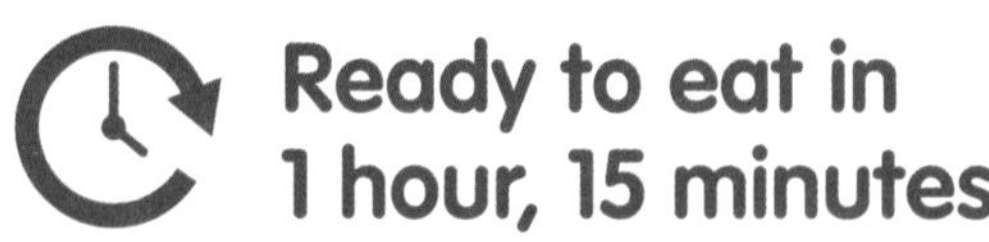

Ready to eat in 1 hour, 15 minutes

Gather Your Kitchen Tools

Large rimmed baking sheet

Parchment paper

Measuring cups and spoons

Large bowl

Silicone spatula

Oven mitts

One super fun way to eat granola is to make a yogurt parfait. It's easy! To a bowl, add a couple scoops of your favorite yogurt, pour in enough granola to cover the yogurt, add a few berries or fruit slices, and repeat until you have 3 or 4 layers or the bowl is nearly full.

Make Your Best-Ever Granola

> To **toss** means to mix ingredients together by lifting them up with the silicone spatula and letting them drop over and over again until everything is evenly combined.

1. Heat the oven to 300°F. Line a rimmed baking sheet with parchment paper by following the directions on page 21.
2. In a large bowl, combine the oil, maple syrup and salt, following the directions on page 17 and 18 to measure liquids and dry ingredients. Add the oats, coconut, sunflower seeds and pumpkin seeds and toss with a silicone spatula to evenly coat everything with the sugary mixture.
3. Spread the mixture out evenly onto the prepared baking sheet.
4. Place the baking sheet in the oven. As the granola bakes, stir it every 15 minutes. The granola is done when it's light golden brown and dry, about 45 to 55 minutes.
5. Remove the pan from the oven and let it cool completely before eating. Store in an airtight container at room temperature for up to 2 weeks.

Granola Bark

Melt 8 ounces of chopped dark chocolate in a microwave on high, stirring with a silicone spatula every 20 seconds until melted. Spread the melted chocolate onto parchment paper. Scatter granola over the chocolate. Refrigerate until set, about 20 minutes. Break into pieces and enjoy! Refrigerate this tasty treat for up to 1 week.

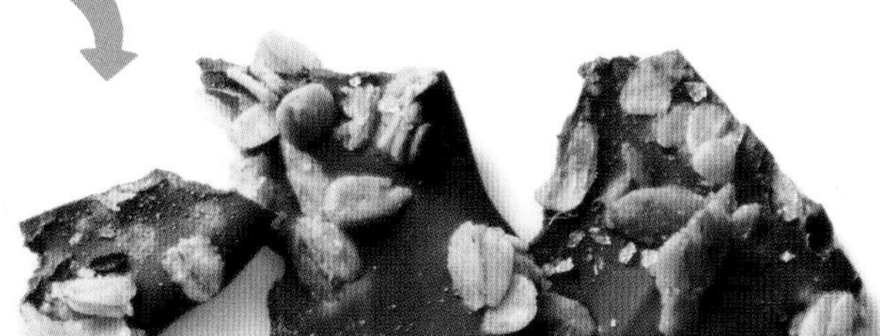

Ooey-Gooey Cinnamon Rolls

Prepare Your Ingredients

Makes 9 rolls

Ready to eat in 50 minutes

Cinnamon Rolls

Butter, for the pan

All-purpose flour, for sprinkling

1 pound pizza dough

3 tablespoons plus 4½ teaspoons unsalted butter, divided, at room temperature

¼ cup packed light brown sugar

1½ teaspoons ground cinnamon

Glaze

1 cup confectioners' sugar

2 tablespoons milk

Kosher salt

Hey, did you see that movie all about cinnamon rolls?
HA HA HA
At the end, it has a big twist!

Gather Your Kitchen Tools

8- by 8-inch baking pan

Large cutting board (optional)

Rolling pin

Ruler

Silicone spatula

Knife

Aluminum foil

Medium bowl

Oven mitts

Wire rack

Make Your Ooey-Gooey Cinnamon Rolls

1. Heat the oven to 375°F. Grease the baking pan with butter by following the directions on page 22.

2. You'll need some room to work, so clear a big space on the counter or get out a large cutting board. Sprinkle flour over your work surface and the rolling pin to prevent the dough from sticking.

3. Roll out the ball of pizza dough into a 12- by 15-inch rectangle by following the directions on page 23.

4. Using a silicone spatula, spread 3 tablespoons of the butter over the dough, then sprinkle it with the brown sugar and cinnamon.

5. Starting at the long side of the rectangle, roll the dough into a tight log shape. Cut the log into nine even pieces. Place each piece on your pan, with a cut side facing up. Dollop the top of each with ½ teaspoon of the remaining butter. Cover the pan with foil.

6. Put the pan in the oven and bake for 20 minutes. Remove the foil and continue to bake until the tops of the rolls are golden brown, another 15 to 20 minutes.

7. While the rolls are baking, make the glaze: In a medium bowl, combine the confectioners' sugar, milk and a pinch of salt. Using a silicone spatula, mix until smooth.

8. When the rolls are done, remove them from the oven and cool on a wire rack for a few minutes. Drizzle them with the glaze (turn the page for tips). Enjoy them warm!

How to Drizzle a Glaze

Drizzling glaze is a fun way to decorate rolls! Use a silicone spatula to scoop up some glaze. Then hold the spatula just over your rolls and allow the glaze to slowly drip down. Try drizzling a zigzag pattern or swirls—whatever you like best!

What Is Pumpkin Pie Spice?
Pumpkin pie spice is a blend of some of autumn's coziest scents and flavors! It typically includes ground cinnamon, ginger, nutmeg, allspice and cloves.
Chocolate Chip Pump-kid Bread page 46

Chocolate Chip Pump-kid Bread

Prepare Your Ingredients

Nonstick cooking spray, for the pan

1¾ cups all-purpose flour

1 teaspoon baking powder

½ teaspoon baking soda

1½ teaspoons pumpkin pie spice

½ teaspoon kosher salt

½ cup (1 stick) unsalted butter, melted

1 cup canned pure pumpkin puree (not pumpkin pie filling)

½ cup granulated sugar

¼ cup packed brown sugar

2 large eggs

2 tablespoons milk

2 teaspoons grated fresh ginger

1 teaspoon pure vanilla extract

½ cup plus 2 tablespoons bittersweet chocolate chips, divided

Ready to eat in 1 hour, 10 minutes

Gather Your Kitchen Tools

8½- by 4½-inch loaf pan

Parchment paper

2 large bowls

Measuring cups and spoons

Whisk

Can opener

Silicone spatula

Oven mitts

Wooden pick

Wire rack

Bread knife

Make Your Chocolate Chip Pump-kid Bread

1. Heat the oven to 350°F.

2. Lightly coat the loaf pan with nonstick cooking spray. Line the pan with parchment paper, leaving a 2-inch overhang on the two long sides. Lightly coat the paper with cooking spray.

3. In a large bowl, whisk together the flour, baking powder, baking soda, pumpkin pie spice and salt; set aside.

If the butter is still hot when you mix in the eggs, the eggs could cook. That would make scrambled-egg bread, which would be pretty gross!

4. In another large bowl, whisk together the melted butter, pumpkin, granulated sugar and brown sugar (this will help cool the butter if it is still hot). Whisk in the eggs, milk, ginger and vanilla.

5. Add the dry flour mixture to the wet mixture and use a silicone spatula to combine. Fold in ½ cup of chocolate chips.

6. Transfer the batter to the prepared pan and scatter the remaining chocolate chips on top.

To **fold** means to gently add one ingredient to another using a folding motion with a silicone spatula.

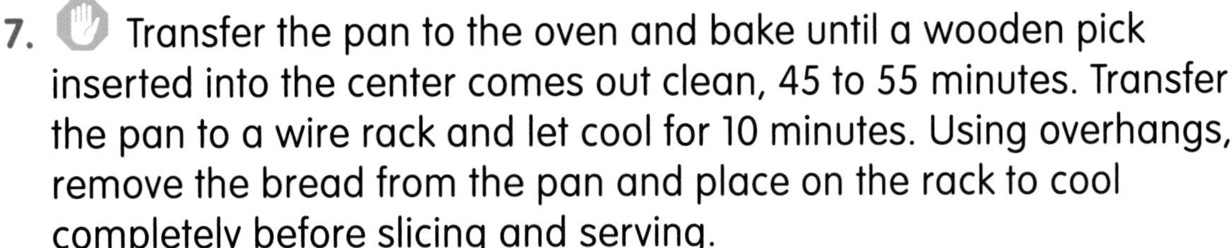

7. Transfer the pan to the oven and bake until a wooden pick inserted into the center comes out clean, 45 to 55 minutes. Transfer the pan to a wire rack and let cool for 10 minutes. Using overhangs, remove the bread from the pan and place on the rack to cool completely before slicing and serving.

Super-Simple Smoothies

Prepare Your Ingredients

Blackberry Blast

¼ cup milk of your choice

½ cup plain yogurt

2 cups blackberries, fresh or frozen

Strawberry-Raspberry

¼ cup milk of your choice

½ cup plain yogurt

1 cup raspberries, fresh or frozen

1 cup strawberries, stems removed, fresh or frozen

Creamy Peach

¼ cup milk of your choice

½ cup plain yogurt

2 cups chopped peaches or nectarines, fresh or frozen

Serves 1

Ready to eat in 5 minutes

Gather Your Kitchen Tools

Cutting board

Knife

Measuring cups

Blender

Silicone spatula, if needed

Tall glass

Spoon

Straw

TIP Freeze fresh fruits and veggies overnight to make your smoothies extra chilly.

Make Your Super-Simple Smoothies

1. In a blender, add the ingredients in the order they are listed.

2. Put the lid on the blender and puree until the ingredients are smooth. If needed, turn off the blender and scrape down the sides with a silicone spatula. Replace the lid and continue to blend.

3. Pour the smoothie into a tall glass and serve with a spoon and straw.

To **blend** means to mix together two or more ingredients very well, using a spoon, whisk, mixer or blender.

To **puree** means to mash food until very smooth using a food processor or blender.

Freezy Fruit Pops
WOW
Did you know you can freeze your smoothies?!

Cool Sweet Treats

Freezy Fruit Pops

Instead of pouring your smoothie into a glass to drink, make an ice pop! After blending, pour the smoothie into ice-pop molds, then insert sticks and freeze. To make layered ice pops, pour two flavors into each mold.

Aquarium Smoothies

Make your smoothie into a work of art by pressing thin slices of fruit against the inside of a clear glass. You can use a wooden skewer to push the fruit closer to the bottom of the glass. Then, carefully spoon the smoothie into the cup, and you'll be left with a colorful drink decorated with a pretty pattern of fresh fruit!

Two-Sides Smoothies

Give your smoothie a cool, colorful effect! Take two smoothies that are different colors, like strawberry and raspberry, and fill a clear cup halfway with one and then fill the rest of the cup with the other. Bonus: You get twice as much flavor!

Always Make Super Smoothies!

For the best results, add your ingredients to the blender in this order:

1. Liquid ingredients
2. Soft fruits and veggies
3. Leafy greens
4. Hard ingredients like seeds and frozen fruits and veggies. Then blend away!

page 54

YUM!

page 56

page 60

page 62

page 66

page 68

page 72

page 74

- Chapter 3 -

Tasty Lunches & Dinners

Who doesn't like pizza?

A weir-dough!

HA HA HA

HA HA

Sandwiches!

Tostadas!

Pasta!

Pizza!

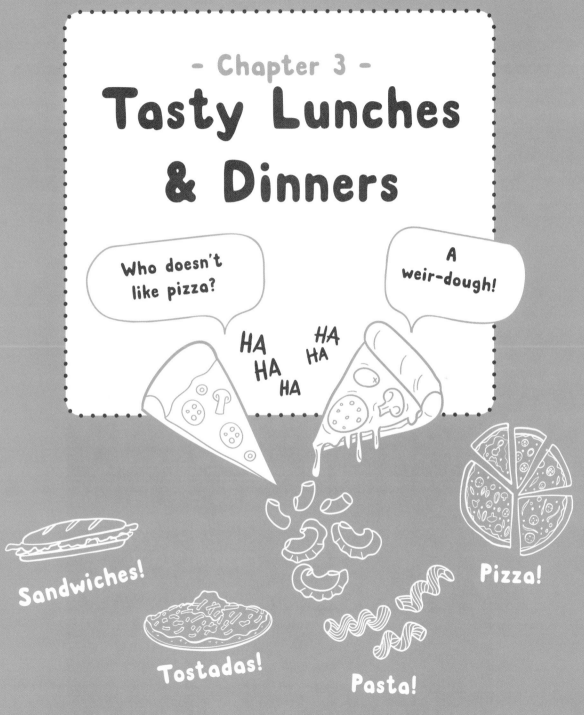

Traffic-Stopping Sandwiches

Prepare Your Ingredients

Sandwich bread slices

Baby spinach

Cheddar cheese slices

Salami slices

Serves as many as you like

Ready to eat in 10 minutes

Gather Your Kitchen Tools

Small circle cookie cutter or bottle cap

Make Your Traffic-Stopping Sandwiches

1. On one slice of bread, place a horizontal row of baby spinach, then a row of Cheddar across the middle and a row of salami along the bottom.

2. Using a cookie cutter or bottle cap, cut three holes in another slice of bread, then place that slice on top of your sandwich. Start your engines!

HA HA HA
What did the traffic light do when it saw its crush?
It turned red!
HA HA

Broccoli-Cheddar Blankies

Prepare Your Ingredients

All-purpose flour, for sprinkling

4 slices bacon

4 ounces sharp Cheddar cheese, grated (about 1 cup)

¼ cup sour cream

2 scallions, sliced

¼ teaspoon kosher salt

¼ teaspoon pepper

1 (10 ounce) package frozen broccoli florets, thawed

1 pound pizza dough

Extra virgin olive oil

Brushing oil on the dough helps it get crispy and golden brown in the oven.

Serves 8

Ready to eat in 45 minutes

Gather Your Kitchen Tools

Measuring cups and spoons

Plate

Paper towel

Rimmed baking sheet

Parchment paper

Large cutting board (if needed)

Large nonstick skillet

Tongs

Large bowl

Silicone spatula

Ruler

Pizza cutter

Pastry brush

Oven mitts

Make Your Broccoli-Cheddar Blankies

1. Heat the oven to 400°F. Line a plate with paper towels. Line a baking sheet with parchment paper.

2. Sprinkle some flour over a clean counter or large cutting board to roll out the pizza dough, using the directions on page 23. The flour keeps the dough from sticking.

3. Cook the bacon in the skillet on medium until crisp, 6 to 8 minutes. Transfer the bacon to the paper towel–lined plate using tongs.

4. Once the bacon has cooled, break the strips into pieces.

5. In a large bowl, combine the Cheddar, sour cream, scallions, salt and pepper. Using a silicone spatula, fold in the broccoli and bacon.

6. On the floured surface, stretch and press the dough to form a 14-inch circle. Using a pizza cutter, divide the dough into 8 triangles.

7. Spread the broccoli mixture over the triangles. Starting at the wide end, wrap the filling in its dough blankie like you see in the photo on the next page. (Some filling will peek out!)

8. Place the blankies onto the prepared baking sheet. Using a pastry brush, brush oil over the blankies.

9. Bake until the blankies turn golden brown, 20 to 25 minutes.

Save It for Later!

These blankies can be prepared and refrigerated (unbaked) for up to 1 day. So if you want to eat only some of them now, you can save the rest to bake tomorrow.

Broccoli-Cheddar
Blankies
page 56
What do you do when your blankie falls off?
You re-cover!

Dad Jokes
Mac and Cheese
page 60

Dad Jokes Mac and Cheese

Prepare Your Ingredients

Kosher salt

2 cloves garlic, crushed

4 tablespoons (½ stick) unsalted butter

¼ cup all-purpose flour

2½ cups whole milk

12 ounces Cheddar cheese, grated (about 3 cups)

8 ounces yellow American cheese, cut into cubes

16-ounce box elbow macaroni

Serves 10

Ready to eat in 35 minutes

Gather Your Kitchen Tools

Large pasta pot

Measuring cups and spoons

Garlic press

Large saucepan

Silicone spatula

Whisk

Colander

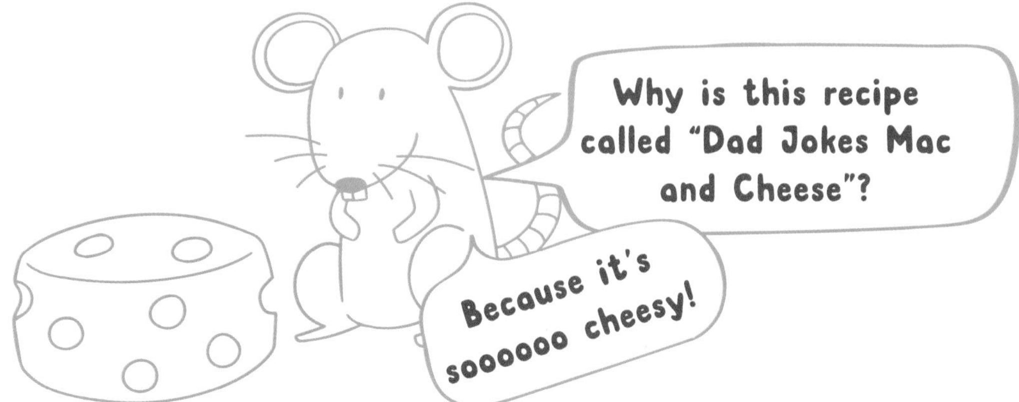

Why is this recipe called "Dad Jokes Mac and Cheese"?
Because it's soooooo cheesy!

Make Your Dad Jokes Mac and Cheese

1. Fill a large pot with water and bring to a boil. Add about a tablespoon of salt, then the pasta and cook according to package directions. Set the pot on high and bring to a boil.

To **boil** means to cook in hot, bubbling water

2. Meanwhile, using a garlic press, press the garlic into a large saucepan. Add the butter and melt on medium. Sprinkle the flour over the melted butter mixture and cook, stirring constantly with a silicone spatula, for 1 minute.

3. Reduce the heat under the butter mixture to medium-low. While whisking, slowly pour the milk into the saucepan. Mix in ½ teaspoon of salt. Increase heat to medium and cook the sauce, stirring occasionally, until it starts to thicken, about 2 minutes.

4. Add the Cheddar and American cheeses a handful at a time, stirring with a silicone spatula. When the cheese melts, add the next handful. Remove the pot from the heat.

5. Add the pasta to the saucepan with the cheese sauce and mix with the spatula until the pasta is fully coated in the sauce. Season with additional salt, if needed. Enjoy it while it's hot!

Totally Twisted Pasta with Cherry Tomato Sauce

Prepare Your Ingredients

12 ounces gemelli, fusilli or rotini pasta

½ sweet onion, very thinly sliced

¼ cup red wine vinegar

3 tablespoons extra virgin olive oil

½ teaspoon kosher salt

½ teaspoon pepper

1 pound cherry tomatoes, halved

2 tablespoons tarragon leaves

3 ounces fresh mozzarella

Serves 4

Ready to eat in 30 minutes

Gather Your Kitchen Tools

Large pasta pot

Colander

Large bowl

Measuring cups and spoons

Silicone spatula

Good to Know: Gemelli Pasta

Gemelli is the Italian word for "twins," which explains this pasta's shape. Gemelli pasta is made of two pasta strands twisted together! Don't have gemelli pasta on hand? Use fusilli or rotini, which are other great twisty pasta shapes!

Make Your Totally Twisted Pasta with Cherry Tomato Sauce

The veggies sit for 15 minutes so they can soak up all the flavors you mixed them with. That's called "marinating."

1. Fill a large pot with water and bring to a boil. Add about a tablespoon of salt, then the pasta and cook according to package directions. Carefully drain the pasta.

2. In a large bowl, toss the onion with the vinegar, oil, salt and pepper with a silicone spatula. Add the tomatoes and toss them too. Allow the tomato mixture to sit for at least 15 minutes, tossing a couple of times.

3. Add the pasta to the tomato mixture and toss to combine. Transfer to a platter and sprinkle with fresh tarragon. Tear the mozzarella and scatter it on top.

Where does the spaghetti go to dance?
The meatball!
Ha!
Ha!
Ha!
Ha!
Ha!

Totally Twisted
Pasta with Cherry
Tomato Sauce
page 62

There are endless ways to top a pizza! Try adding thinly sliced ham and a favorite salad green, pepperoni and honey, a drizzle of pesto or a mix of cheeses like mozzarella and Cheddar or Colby and Jack cheese.
GH
The Queen's Pizza page 66

The Queen's Pizza

Prepare Your Ingredients

1 pound pizza dough

¾ cup marinara sauce

6 ounces fresh mozzarella cheese

¼ cup grated Parmesan cheese

¼ cup packed basil leaves

Pizza History

According to cooking legend, 150 years ago this kind of pizza was named for the queen of Italy, Margherita Maria Teresa Giovanna. She *loved* it, and the name "Margherita Pizza" has stuck all the way to today.

Gather Your Kitchen Tools

Measuring cups and spoons

Baking sheet

Parchment paper

Ruler

Spoon

Silicone spatula

Oven mitts

Pizza cutter

Make Your Queen's Pizza

1. Place a baking sheet into a cold oven. Heat the oven to 475°F.

2. Unroll about 16 inches of parchment paper. Cut off the piece and set it on your work surface.

3. Place the pizza dough on the sheet of parchment paper. Stretch and press the dough to form a 14-inch circle. Pinch around the edges to make a slight rim. Use the back of a spoon to spread the sauce on the dough, keeping the rim sauce-free (See how to spread sauce on a pizza, page 24). Pull apart the mozzarella and put it on top in a single layer. Sprinkle the pizza with Parmesan cheese.

4. Use the parchment paper to lift the pizza and carefully lower it onto the hot baking sheet in the oven.

5. Bake until the bottom is crisp and golden brown, 15 to 20 minutes. Remove the pizza from the oven and top with fresh basil. Allow to cool slightly before cutting and serving.

Tex-Mex Tostadas

Prepare Your Ingredients

Canola oil

4 8-inch flour tortillas

4 ounces pepper Jack cheese

1 15-ounce can refried beans

¼ cup salsa

1 ounce Spanish chorizo, thinly sliced

Avocado, lettuce and tomatoes, for topping

Lime wedges

cilantro, chopped, for garnish

What's a bean's favorite kind of show?
A podcast!

Gather Your Kitchen Tools

2 rimmed baking sheets

Small bowl

Pastry brush

Tongs

Box grater

Parchment paper

Can opener

Spoon

Oven mitts

Measuring cups and spoons

Knife

Cutting board

Make Your Tex-Mex Tostadas

1. Place 2 rimmed baking sheets in the cold oven, then heat the oven to 425°F.

2. Pour a little canola oil into a small bowl. Using a pastry brush, lightly brush the tortillas on both sides with the oil. Place the tortillas on the hot baking sheets. Bake for 4 minutes, then use tongs to carefully flip, and bake until the tortillas are crisp, about 4 minutes more.

3. While the tortillas are baking, coarsely shred the pepper Jack cheese using the box grater. Set 2 large sheets of parchment paper on a work surface.

4. Using tongs, gently remove the tortillas from the oven and place them onto the parchment paper (2 tortillas per sheet). Leave the pans in the oven and do not turn the oven off.

5. Use a spoon to spread the refried beans on the tortillas, following the directions on page 24, then spread the salsa on top. Divide the chorizo and the cheese among the tortillas.

6. Use the parchment paper to lift the tostadas and carefully return them to the pans in the oven. Bake until the cheese melts, about 5 minutes.

7. While the tortillas are baking, slice the avocado and lettuce and chop the tomatoes.

8. Top the tostadas with the vegetables, squeeze fresh lime juice over the top and garnish with cilantro.

Tex-Mex
Tostadas
page 68
"Tex-Mex" is short for
"Texan" and "Mexican."
Tex-Mex food comes
from the area where
the United States
and Mexico meet.
GH

Crunchy Chicken Sandwich page 72
Fun Food Fact!
George Washington was such a pickle lover that he grew and saved seeds from more than 400 varieties of pickling cucumbers.

Crunchy Chicken Sandwich

Prepare Your Ingredients

2 8- to 12-ounce packages breaded chicken tenders

⅓ cup mayonnaise

1 tablespoon yellow mustard

1 tablespoon ketchup

1 large loaf Italian bread

5 to 10 leaves romaine lettuce

2 plum tomatoes, sliced

3 half-sour pickles, sliced

Ready to eat in 30 minutes

Gather Your Kitchen Tools

Plate

Small bowl

Spoon

Serrated knife

Colander

Paper towels

Silicone spatula

Why did the dinosaur cross the road?
Because chickens weren't around yet!

Ha!
Ha!
Ha!
Ha!
Ha!

Make Your Crunchy Chicken Sandwich

1. Follow the microwave cooking instructions on the package of chicken tenders. (If you want to bake them in the oven, have an adult help out.)

2. While the chicken is cooking, combine the mayonnaise, yellow mustard and ketchup in a small bowl. Use a spoon to mix it all together. Set aside.

3. Slice the Italian bread in half, lengthwise. Remove the hot chicken tenders from the microwave and let cool.

4. Wash the lettuce leaves and pat them dry with paper towels.

5. Once the chicken tenders are cooled, it's time to build the sandwiches!
   - Using the silicone spatula, spread the sauce evenly on the bottom half of the Italian bread.
   - Layer the rest of your ingredients on top of the sauce: first the lettuce leaves, then the tomatoes, then the chicken tenders, then the pickles.

6. Top your sandwich with the other half of Italian bread. Cut the huge sandwich into 10 smaller sandwiches and enjoy!

Why Wash Your Lettuce?

Lettuce, and other fruit and vegetables, can carry gross bacteria that can make people sick, so a good rinse is important. Place a few leaves at a time in a colander under a gentle stream of cool water, and make sure to rinse both sides. Then pat the leaves dry with clean paper towels. Now they're ready to eat!

Best-Ever Flank Steak with Orange Chimichurri Marinade & Even Better Broccoli

Prepare Your Ingredients

Orange Chimichurri Marinade

1 small orange

1 teaspoon grated lime zest plus 1 tablespoon lime juice

1 scallion, finely chopped

2 tablespoons extra virgin olive oil

½ cup chopped fresh cilantro

¼ cup chopped fresh parsley

Flank Steak

1½ to 2 pounds beef flank steak

½ teaspoon kosher salt

½ teaspoon pepper

Grilled Broccoli

2 tablespoons unsalted butter, at room temperature

2 teaspoons grated lemon zest plus 1 tablespoon lemon juice

1 small clove garlic, pressed

1 teaspoon honey

¾ teaspoon kosher salt, divided

¾ teaspoon pepper, divided

1½ pounds broccoli crowns, cut lengthwise into 1-inch-thick slices

2 tablespoons extra virgin olive oil

Serves 4–6

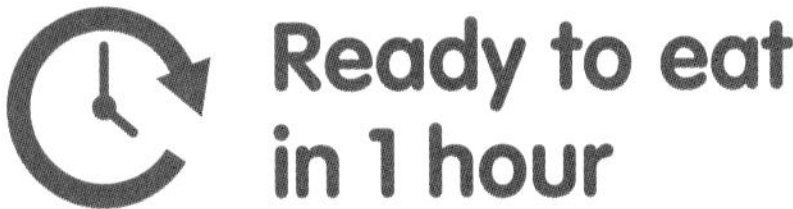
Ready to eat in 1 hour

Gather Your Kitchen Tools

Vegetable peeler

Knife

Medium bowl

Measuring cups and spoons

Wooden spoon

Large resealable plastic bag

Grill

Tongs

Cutting board

Large bowl

Pastry brush

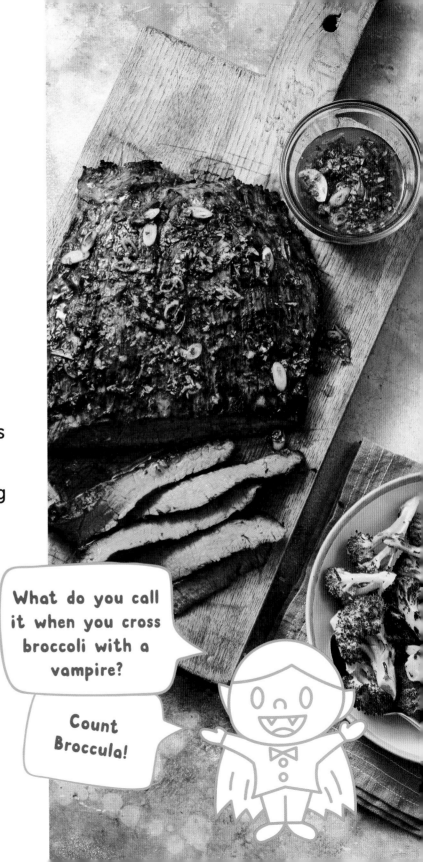

What do you call it when you cross broccoli with a vampire?

Count Broccula!

Flip the page to find out how to make this!

Make the Marinade

1. Using a vegetable peeler, remove 2 large strips of zest from the orange. Finely chop the zest and place in a medium bowl. Squeeze in 2 tablespoons of orange juice by following the directions on page 20.

2. Add the lime zest and juice along with the scallion, olive oil, cilantro and parsley and mix with a wooden spoon to combine.

Make the Steak

1. Pour the marinade in a large resealable plastic bag. Add the steak, then seal the bag. Turn the bag over and over to coat the steak in the marinade. Let the steak sit out at room temperature in marinade for at least 30 minutes or refrigerate it for up to 2 hours.

2. Heat the grill to medium-high. Remove the steak from the marinade. Season with the salt and pepper and grill, covered, for 4 minutes.

3. Use tongs to turn the steak and grill, covered, to desired doneness, 3 to 5 minutes more for medium-rare (135°F), depending on thickness. Transfer the steak to a cutting board and let it rest for 10 minutes before slicing it. Leave the grill on for the broccoli if you're not grilling the steak and broccoli at the same time.

4. Slice the steak into ½-inch-thick slices.

Make the Broccoli

1. In a large bowl, combine the butter, lemon zest and juice. Using a garlic press, add the garlic then add the honey and ¼ teaspoon each of salt and pepper. Set aside.

2. Brush the broccoli with the olive oil and sprinkle with ½ teaspoon each of salt and pepper.

3. With the grill on medium-high, grill the broccoli until it is lightly charred and just barely tender, 2 to 3 minutes per side. Transfer the grilled broccoli to the large bowl with the lemon butter.

4. Toss the broccoli in the lemon butter mixture until it's coated and serve the broccoli with the steak.

The butter will melt as it is tossed with hot broccoli!

Easy to Make Marinades!

There are lots of different marinades you can make for this steak, like the tasty one below! Just mix all the ingredients together in a plastic bag, add the steak and let it sit at room temperature for 30 minutes or in the refrigerator for 2 hours.

Balsamic-Rosemary Marinade

3 tablespoons balsamic vinegar
2 tablespoons extra virgin olive oil
2 cloves garlic, thinly sliced
1 tablespoon whole-grain mustard
1 tablespoon coriander seeds
1 tablespoon peppercorns
1 sprig rosemary

YUM!
page 80
page 84
YUM YUM
page 86
page 90
Yum! yum!
page 92
page 94

- Chapter 4 -

Super Snacks

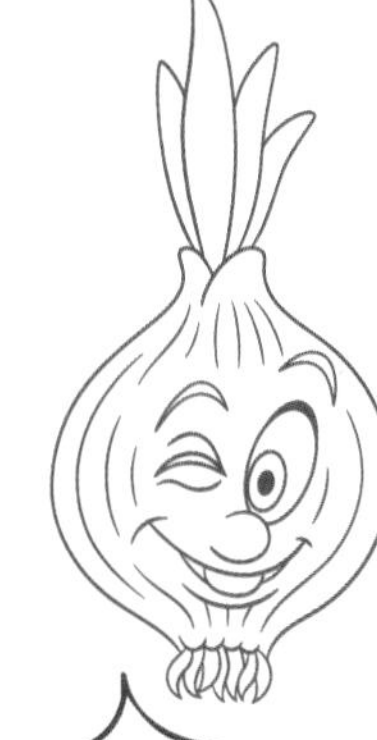

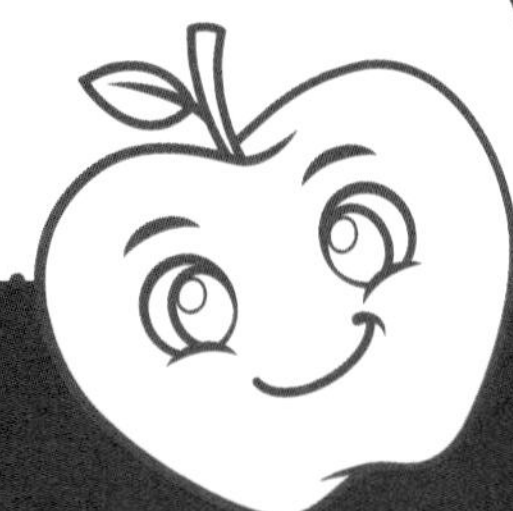

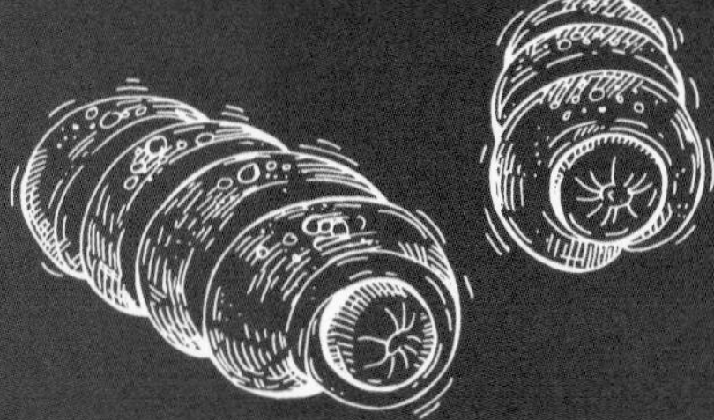

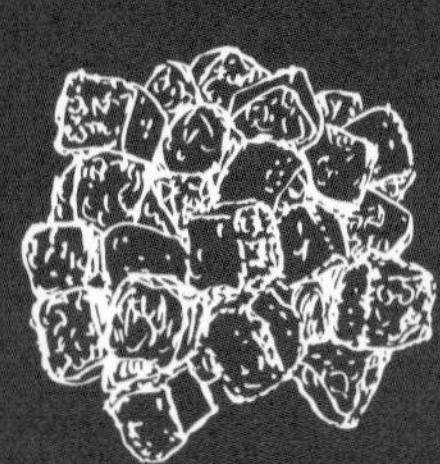

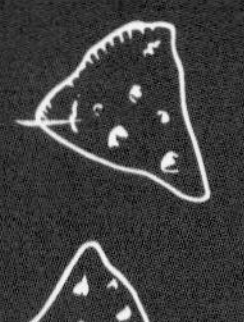

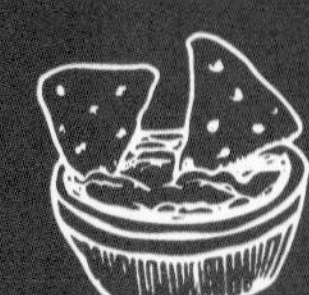

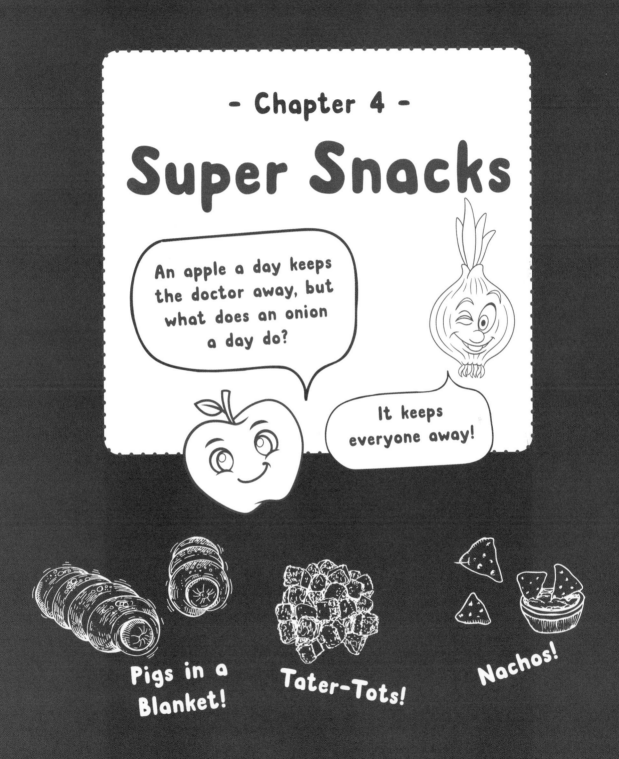

Cozy Pigs in Blankets

Prepare Your Ingredients

2 8-count packages refrigerated crescent roll dough

2 tablespoons Dijon mustard, plus more for dipping

1 12-ounce package cocktail franks

1 large egg

1 tablespoon water

1 teaspoon caraway seeds

Makes 32

Ready to eat in 45 minutes

Gather Your Kitchen Tools

Baking sheet

Parchment paper

Cutting board

Pastry brush

Pizza cutter

Small bowl

Measuring spoons

Fork

Oven mitts

People love these snacks so much, there's a holiday to celebrate them. April 24th is National Pigs in a Blanket day!

Make Your Cozy Pigs in Blankets

1. Heat the oven to 375°F. Line a baking sheet with parchment paper.

2. Pop open the dough tubes and unroll the dough onto a cutting board. Using a pastry brush, brush mustard over the dough. Rinse the pastry brush and set aside.

3. Use a pizza cutter to cut each triangle in half lengthwise to create two skinnier triangles.

4. Place one cocktail frank on the wide end of each dough triangle, then roll the frank up in the dough. Arrange the pigs in blankets on the prepared baking sheet in two concentric circles, making sure the dough in both circles touch. See the photo on the next page.

5. In a small bowl, beat the egg with 1 tablespoon of water. Brush the egg wash over the dough and sprinkle with the caraway seeds.

6. Bake until golden brown, 18 to 22 minutes. Serve with extra mustard for dipping.

It's Alive!

When you pop open a tube of dough it starts to *grow*! That's what it looks like anyway, but it's not really growing. The dough is packed into the tube so tightly that when you open it, it starts sucking in air and getting bigger. It's a little like when you squish a sponge in your hand and then open your hand back up and the sponge expands.

Cozy Pigs in Blankets page 80
What do you call a pig that's no fun?
HA HA HA
A boar!

How Do Tots Get So Crispy?

Some foods, like tater tots, are usually deep-fried in hot oil, giving them a crispy, brown outside. An air fryer uses a fan to blow super-hot air around your food really, really, fast. The food gets that yummy, crispy outside but with way less oil!

Tot-chos page 84

Tot-chos

Prepare Your Ingredients

2 pounds frozen potato tots

½ teaspoon chili powder

½ teaspoon ground cumin

½ teaspoon ground coriander

⅛ teaspoon cayenne (optional)

6 ounces extra-sharp Cheddar cheese, grated (about 1½ cups)

Guacamole, for serving

Gather Your Kitchen Tools

Large bowl

Silicone spatula

Measuring cups and spoons

Air fryer (if you have one) or rimmed baking sheet

Small platter

Aluminum foil

Oven mitts

Make Your Tot-chos

1. In a large bowl, use a silicone spatula to toss the tots with the chili powder, cumin, coriander and cayenne (if you like spicy food!).

2. Heat an air fryer to 400°F. Arrange the tots in a single layer in the air fryer basket and cook until golden, 20 minutes. Or bake in the oven according to the tots' instructions.

3. Remove half of the tots from the air fryer or oven and place on a small platter.

4. Sprinkle the tots with half of the Cheddar, then layer on the rest of the tots. Add the rest of the cheese on top.

5. Cover the tot-chos loosely with foil and let them sit for about 30 seconds. The cheese will melt from the heat of the hot tots. Serve immediately with your favorite guacamole!

What do you use to carry potatoes in?
A tater tote.
HA HA HA
HA HA HA

Nummy Nachos

Prepare Your Ingredients

Serves 6

6 ounces tortilla chips (about 7 cups)

1 15-ounce can low-sodium black beans, rinsed and drained

8 ounces extra-sharp Cheddar cheese, grated (about 2 cups)

1 15-ounce can refried beans

¼ cup sour cream

1 cup romaine lettuce, shredded

½ cup pico de gallo (fresh salsa)

½ cup guacamole (yummy avocado dip)

Ready to eat in 15 minutes

Gather Your Kitchen Tools

Can opener

Large bowl

Silicone spatula

Rimmed baking sheet

Oven mitts

Serving dish

2 large spoons

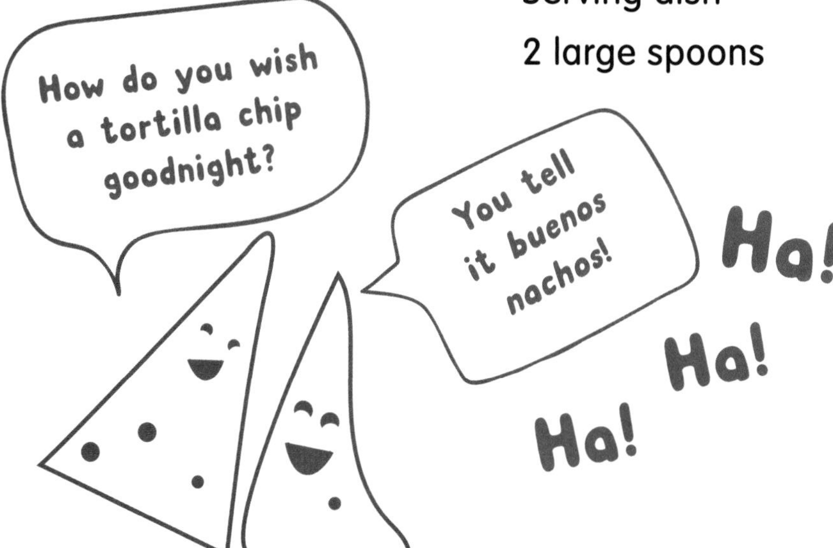

How do you wish a tortilla chip goodnight?
You tell it buenos nachos!
Ha!
Ha!
Ha!

Make Your Nummy Nachos

1. Heat the oven to 450°F.

2. Pour the chips, black beans and half of the Cheddar into a large bowl. Use a silicone spatula to toss the ingredients together, being careful not to break too many chips. (It's totally fine if a few break, though. The melty nacho cheese will fix that!)

3. Pour the chip mix onto a baking sheet. Use a spoon to dollop refried beans on top of the chips, then sprinkle on the rest of the Cheddar.

4. Place the baking sheet into the oven and bake until the cheese has melted, 6 to 7 minutes. Transfer the nachos to a serving dish.

5. Dollop sour cream over the nachos and top with lettuce, pico de gallo and guacamole.

Switch It Up!

Follow the steps for Nummy Nachos but try this variation: Toss shredded cooked chicken with salsa verde (green salsa!). Add the chicken to the chips along with grated Muenster cheese and toss to combine. Spread on a baking sheet, top with more cheese and bake as instructed.

What's a Dollop?

A dollop is a big drop of something gloopy—like the refried beans and sour cream in this recipe. To get a dollop of something, use a large spoon to scoop the ingredient, and then use the back of another spoon to push a glob off and onto your dish!

Nummy
Nachos
page 86

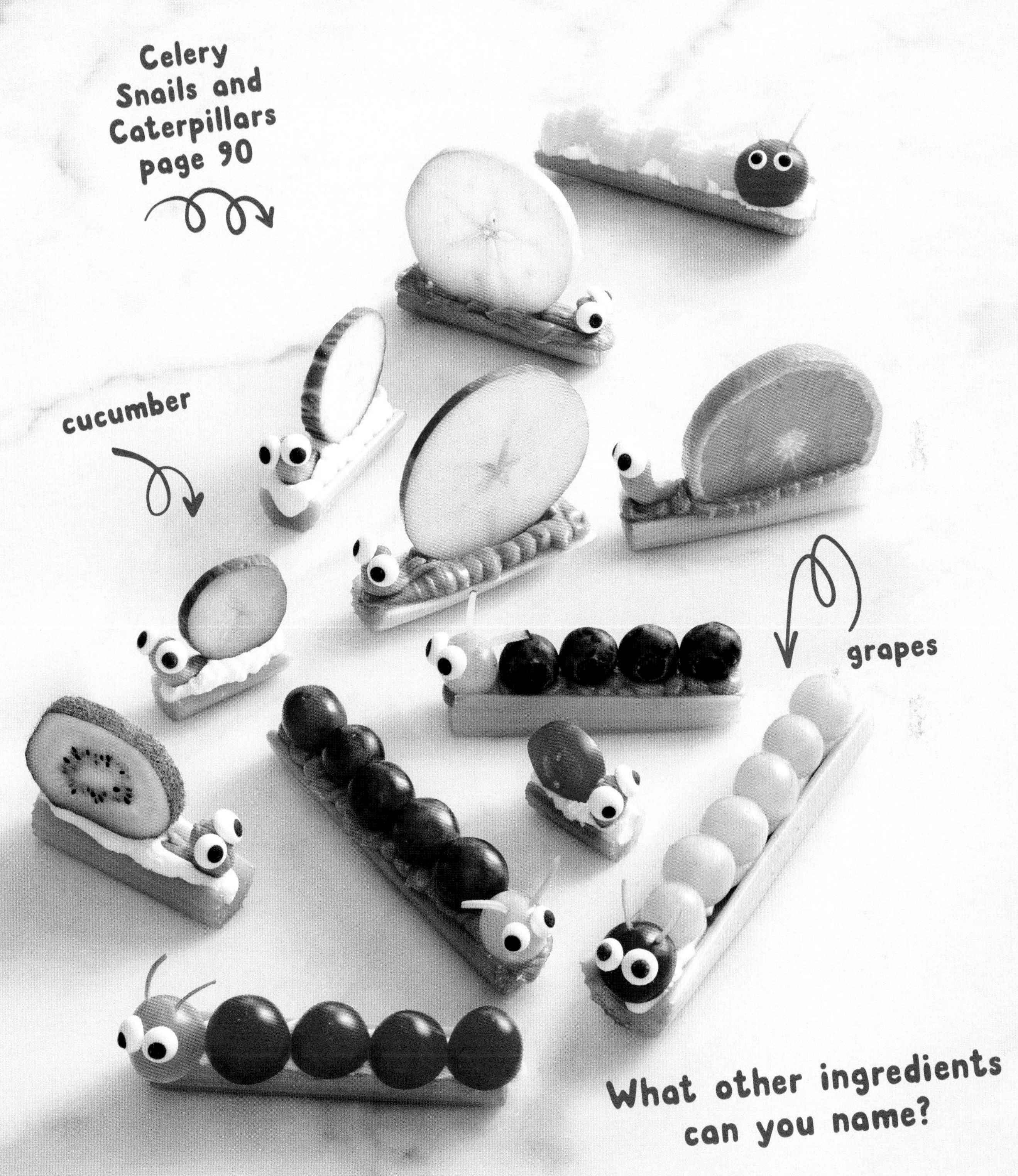
Celery
Snails and
Caterpillars
page 90
cucumber
grapes
What other ingredients
can you name?

Celery Snails & Caterpillars

Prepare Your Ingredients

Snails

Celery ribs, cut to length

Your choice of:

Peanut butter or cream cheese, at room temperature

Apple, sliced into ¼-inch rounds

Orange, sliced into ¼-inch rounds

Kiwi, sliced into ¼-inch rounds

Cucumber, sliced into ¼-inch rounds

Tomato, sliced into ¼-inch rounds

Cashews

Candy eyes or raisins

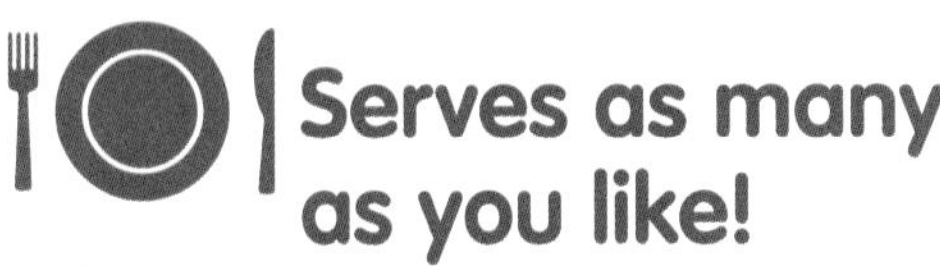

Serves as many as you like!

Ready to eat in 10 minutes

Caterpillars

Celery ribs, cut to length

Peanut butter or cream cheese, at room temperature

Your choice of:

Grapes

Blueberries

Grape tomatoes

Candy eyes or raisins

Celery or radish matchsticks

Gather Your Kitchen Tools

Spoons

Make the Snails 

1. Using a spoon, scoop up a little bit of peanut butter or cream cheese and spread it into the center of the celery rib.
2. Top with a slice of apple, orange, kiwi, cucumber or tomato for the shell and a cashew for the head. Use peanut butter or cream cheese to glue on candy eyes or raisins.

Make the Caterpillars

1. Using a spoon, scoop up a little bit of peanut butter or cream cheese and spread it into the celery.
2. Top with grapes, blueberries or grape tomatoes for the body and head. Use peanut butter or cream cheese to glue on the candy eyes or raisins. Do the same with the celery or radish matchsticks to make the antennae.

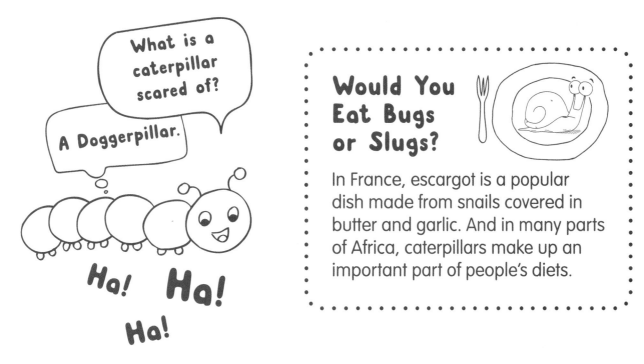

What is a caterpillar scared of?
A Doggerpillar.
Ha! Ha! Ha!

Would You Eat Bugs or Slugs?

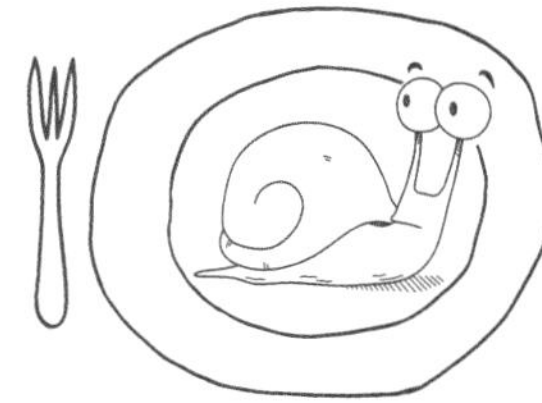

In France, escargot is a popular dish made from snails covered in butter and garlic. And in many parts of Africa, caterpillars make up an important part of people's diets.

Veggie Garden Toast

Prepare Your Ingredients

3 slices bread

1 tablespoon fresh dill, chopped (optional)

½ cup whipped cream cheese

Your choice of:

Veggies, sliced

Microgreens or fresh herbs

HA
HA
HA
What did the flower say to his partner?
I love you a lily more each day!

Serves 3

Ready to eat in 15 minutes

Gather Your Kitchen Tools

Toaster

Small bowl

Measuring cups and spoons

Spoon

Butter knife or Silicone spatula

Make Your Veggie Garden Toast

1. Toast the bread in the toaster.
2. In a small bowl, mix the dill into the whipped cream cheese if you like, then spread the cream cheese on the slices of toast.
3. Arrange your favorite sliced veggies on the toast to form colorful blossoms on a lawn of microgreens and other fresh herbs!

Veggie Garden Toast
My daughter and I developed these and it was her idea to make a dilly cream cheese. She used scissors to "chop" the dill. Use any soft herb you like!
GH
What vegetables can you name in the toast garden?

Fruit Roll Fun!

Prepare Your Ingredients

3 cups hulled strawberries, diced mango or blackberries

2 teaspoons lemon juice

¼ cup sugar

To **hull** a strawberry means to remove the stem. First remove the leaves. Then push a sturdy straw up into the bottom of the berry and pull it all the way through to remove the stem at the top.

Serves 10

Ready to eat in 3 hours plus cooling

Gather Your Kitchen Tools

Rimmed baking sheet

Parchment paper

Blender

Measuring cups and spoons

Offset spatula

Oven mitts

Wire rack

Kitchen shears

Parchment paper

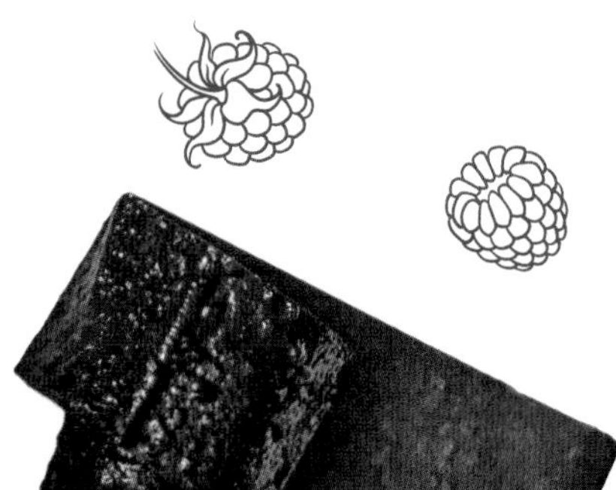

Make Your Fruit Roll Fun

1. Heat the oven to 250°F. Line a baking sheet with parchment paper.
2. In a blender, puree the fruit, lemon juice and sugar until they're almost smooth. With an offset spatula, spread the mixture evenly over the whole prepared baking sheet.

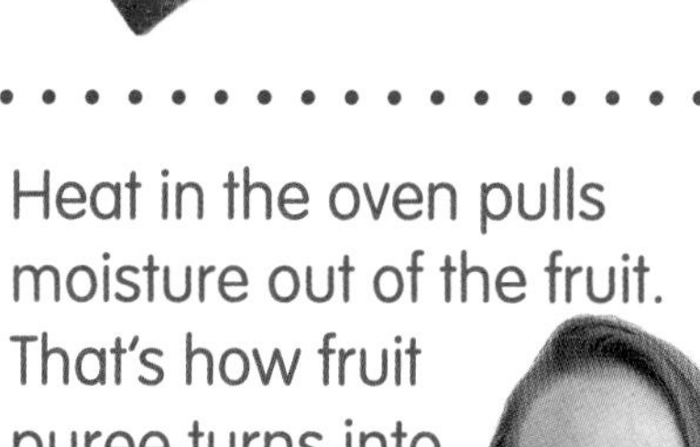

Heat in the oven pulls moisture out of the fruit. That's how fruit puree turns into dried fruit rolls.

3. Bake until the fruit is no longer very sticky but still slightly tacky to the touch, 1½ to 3 hours. Transfer the pan to a wire rack and let it cool for several hours or overnight.
4. Use kitchen shears to cut the fruit (and parchment paper) into 1½-inch strips.
5. Roll up each strip and save them in an airtight container at room temperature. They're good for up to 1 week. When you want to munch them, unroll and remove from parchment paper to enjoy!

Shaping Up to Be Pretty Cool!

Instead of cutting the fruit leather into strips, use small cookie cutters to make cool shapes. Stack between layers of parchment paper to store them, then have fun peeling out different fruity shapes when you're ready for a snack!

YUM YUM

page 98

page 100

page 104

page 106

page 110

page 112

Yum! yum!

YUM!

page 114

page 116

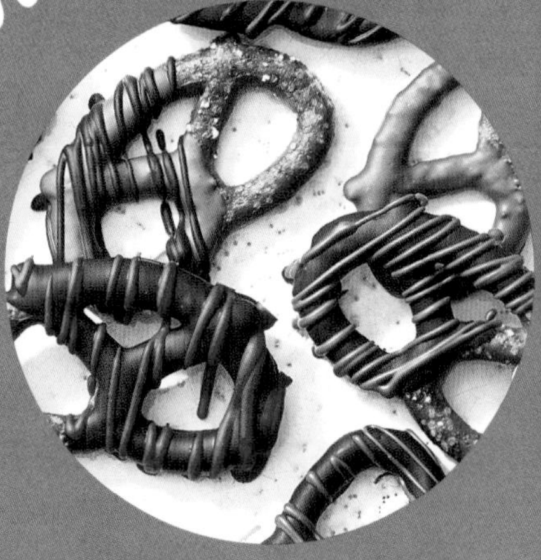
page 120

- Chapter 5 -

Sweet!

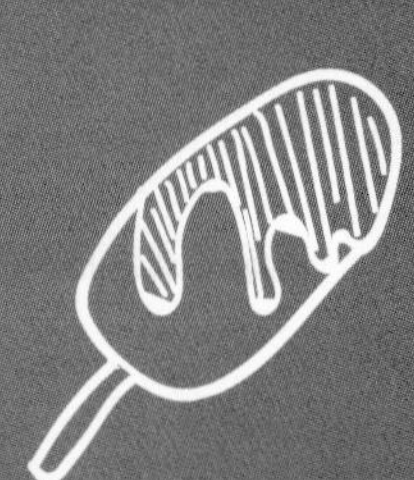

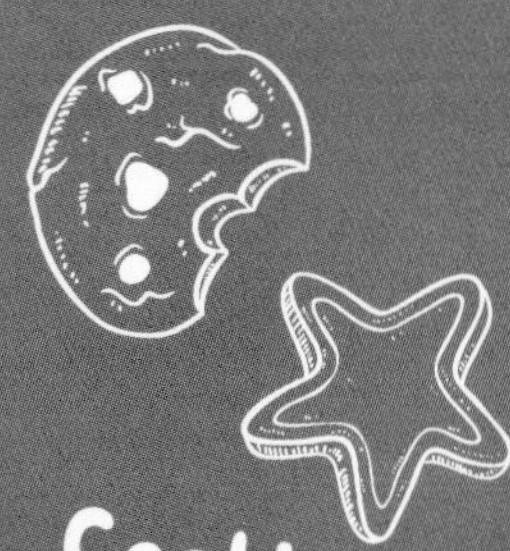

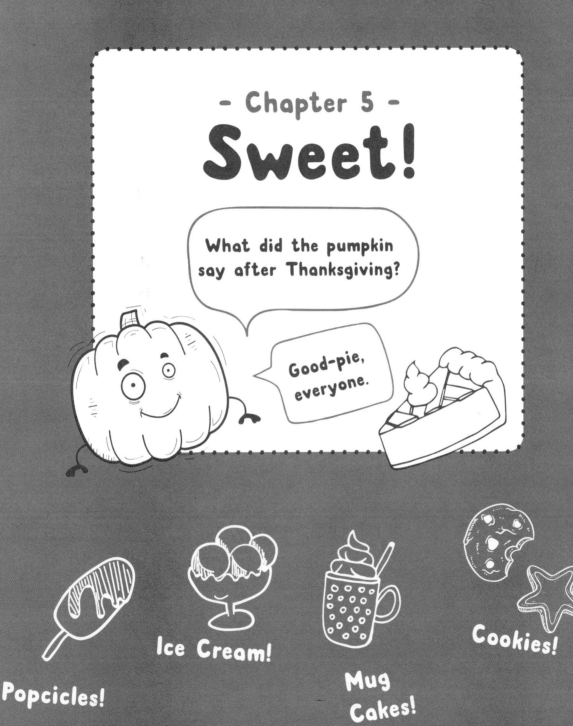

Go Nuts for Nut Butter Cups

Prepare Your Ingredients

1 ripe medium banana

¼ cup of your favorite nut butter like peanut, almond or cashew butter

12 ounces bittersweet chocolate chips

Flaky sea salt, for sprinkling

Serves 24

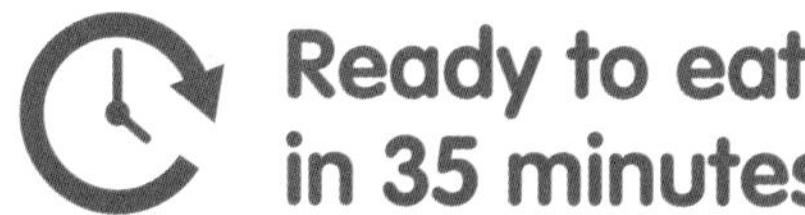

Ready to eat in 35 minutes

Gather Your Kitchen Tools

Mini muffin pan

Mini muffin foil liners

2 small bowls

Fork

Measuring cups and spoons

Silicone spatula

You're Eating Crystals!

Salt is a delicious mineral that forms in crystals. It is used to bring out flavors in dishes and even desserts like cake! It's one of the only crystals you can eat.

Make Your Go Nuts for Nut Butter Cups

1. Line a mini muffin pan with foil liners.
2. In a small bowl, use a fork to mash the banana with the nut butter.
3. Place the chocolate chips in the second small bowl. Microwave on high, stirring with a silicone spatula every 20 seconds until melted.
4. Drop a scant teaspoon of chocolate into each liner, then spoon 1 teaspoon of the banana mixture on top. Top with another teaspoon of chocolate, spreading it to cover the filling.
5. Sprinkle with sea salt and freeze until firm, about 20 minutes. Transfer to an airtight container and refrigerate for up 3 weeks.

What's That Word?

A "scant" of something is just a little less than the amount called for. In this recipe, a scant teaspoon of chocolate is a little less than a teaspoon.

What's the most expensive nut?
The cashew!
HA
HA
HA

One-Bite No-Bake Cookie Cheesecakes

Prepare Your Ingredients

12 ounces cream cheese (1½ packages), at room temperature

3 tablespoons sugar

1 cup cold heavy cream

20 chocolate sandwich cookies

Mini chocolate sandwich cookies, for topping

Gather Your Kitchen Tools

Measuring cups and spoons

Large bowl

Electric mixer

Silicone spatula

12-cup nonstick mini cheesecake pan with removable bottoms

Crush Them Up!

To crush up cookies, put them in a resealable plastic bag, push out all the air and zip it shut. Then run it over with a rolling pin until the cookies are broken up into little pieces.

Make Your One-Bite No-Bake Cookie Cheesecakes

1. In a large bowl, add the cream cheese and sugar. Using an electric mixer, beat the cream cheese and sugar on medium speed until they're smooth.

2. Reduce the mixer speed to low and gradually add the cream. Increase the speed to high and beat until the mixture is thick and stiff, about 2 minutes.

3. Crush and crumble 8 sandwich cookies. Using a silicone spatula, fold the cookie crumbs into the cream cheese mixture.

4. Place the remaining 12 whole sandwich cookies in the cups of the cheesecake pan. Divide the cream-cheese mixture among the cups. Carefully tap the pan on your work surface. Top with the mini sandwich cookies and refrigerate until firm, at least 3 hours and up to 1 day.

Switch It Up!

For One-Bite Strawberry Cheesecakes, replace the sandwich cookies with vanilla wafers and top each cake with a slice of strawberry!

Tapping the pan on your work surface knocks any extra air out of the mixture so it gets into all the nooks and crannies around the cookies.

One-Bite No-Bake Cookie Cheesecakes
page 100

Sure-Fun Sugar Buns page 104
What makes puff pastry puff? Puff pastry is layers of thin dough made from flour, water, and butter. When the oven warms it, the water turns to steam, pushing the layers apart.
CH
Look at how puffy this pastry gets!

Sure-Fun Sugar Buns

Prepare Your Ingredients

¼ cup granulated sugar

1½ teaspoons ground cinnamon, divided

2 tablespoons brown sugar

2 8¼-ounce sheets puff pastry, thawed

10 marshmallows

2 tablespoons unsalted butter, melted

HA
HA
What kind of garden does a baker grow?
A "flour" garden.
HA
HA
HA

Makes 10 buns

Ready to eat in 45 minutes

Gather Your Kitchen Tools

2 small bowls

Measuring cups and spoons

Silicone spatula

Rolling pin

Pizza cutter

Nonstick muffin pan

Oven mitts

Tongs

Serving dish or wire rack

Make Your Sure-Fun Sugar Buns

1. Heat the oven to 375°F.

2. In a small bowl, combine the granulated sugar and 1 teaspoon of the cinnamon using a silicone spatula. In a second small bowl, combine the brown sugar and the remaining ½ teaspoon cinnamon using the same spatula.

3. Sprinkle 1 tablespoon of the granulated sugar mixture onto a clean work surface and place a sheet of puff pastry on top. Set second sheet of puff pastry aside. Sprinkle another tablespoon of the granulated sugar mixture over the top of the pastry. Using a rolling pin, roll over the pastry just once to help the sugar stick. Do the same thing for the other sheet of puff pastry. (You'll have a little bit of the granulated sugar mixture left over).

4. Use a pizza cutter to cut each sheet of pastry into 5 equal strips.

5. Working with 1 strip of dough at a time, dip a marshmallow in the melted butter, then roll the marshmallow in the brown sugar mixture to coat. Place the sugary marshmallow on one end of the pastry strip and roll it up. Pinch the pastry together on one end to create a seam, covering the marshmallow. Repeat with the remaining strips.

6. Place the rolls, seam side down, in the cups of a nonstick muffin pan.

7. Bake until the rolls are golden brown and puffed, 30 to 35 minutes. Immediately use tongs to remove the sugar buns from the pan and transfer to a serving dish or wire rack.

Cocoa Cool Cookie Sandwiches

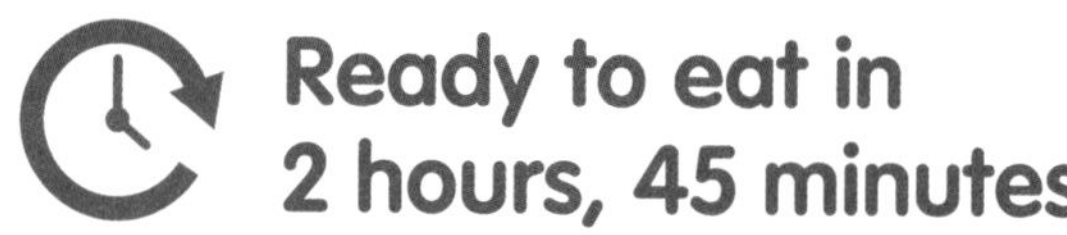

Prepare Your Ingredients

Filling

1/3 cup heavy cream

4 ounces cream cheese

4 ounces white chocolate chips

Cookies

1 cup all-purpose flour

1/2 cup unsweetened cocoa

1/2 teaspoon baking powder

1/2 teaspoon baking soda

1/4 teaspoon kosher salt

3/4 cup sugar

1/2 cup (1 stick) unsalted butter, at room temperature

1 large egg

1/2 teaspoon pure vanilla extract

Gather Your Kitchen Tools

Medium saucepan

Measuring cups and spoons

Whisk

Silicone spatula

2 large bowls

2 baking sheets

Parchment paper

Plastic wrap

Medium bowl

Electric mixer

Oven mitts

Wire rack

Resealable plastic bag

Spoon

Scissors

Make Your Cocoa Cool Cookie Sandwiches

1. In a medium saucepan, combine the heavy cream and the cream cheese and cook on medium-low, whisking, until the cream cheese is melted and combined. Remove from the heat and add the white chocolate, whisking until melted and smooth. Using a silicone spatula, transfer the mixture to a large bowl and let it cool for 10 minutes. Cover and refrigerate until chilled, about 2 hours. Wash the whisk and set aside.

2. Heat the oven to 350°F. Line 2 baking sheets with parchment paper.

3. In a medium bowl, whisk together the flour, cocoa, baking powder, baking soda and salt, following the directions on page 18. Set aside.

4. In the other large bowl, combine the sugar and butter. Using an electric mixer, beat until light and fluffy, then beat in the egg and the vanilla. Turn off the mixer and use a silicone spatula to scrape down the sides of the bowl. Reduce the mixer speed to low and gradually add the flour mixture. Keep mixing until everything is just combined.

5. Drop level teaspoons of your dough onto the prepared baking sheets, spacing them about 1½ inches apart.

6. Bake until the cookies are firm around the edges but slightly soft in the center, 8 to 10 minutes. Let cool on the baking sheets for 5 minutes, then transfer to a wire rack to cool completely.

7. Using an electric mixer, beat the chilled white chocolate filling until fluffy, about 2 minutes. Spoon the filling into a large resealable plastic bag. Snip a ½-inch opening off one corner of the bag, pipe the frosting on half the cookies, and put the other cookies on top.

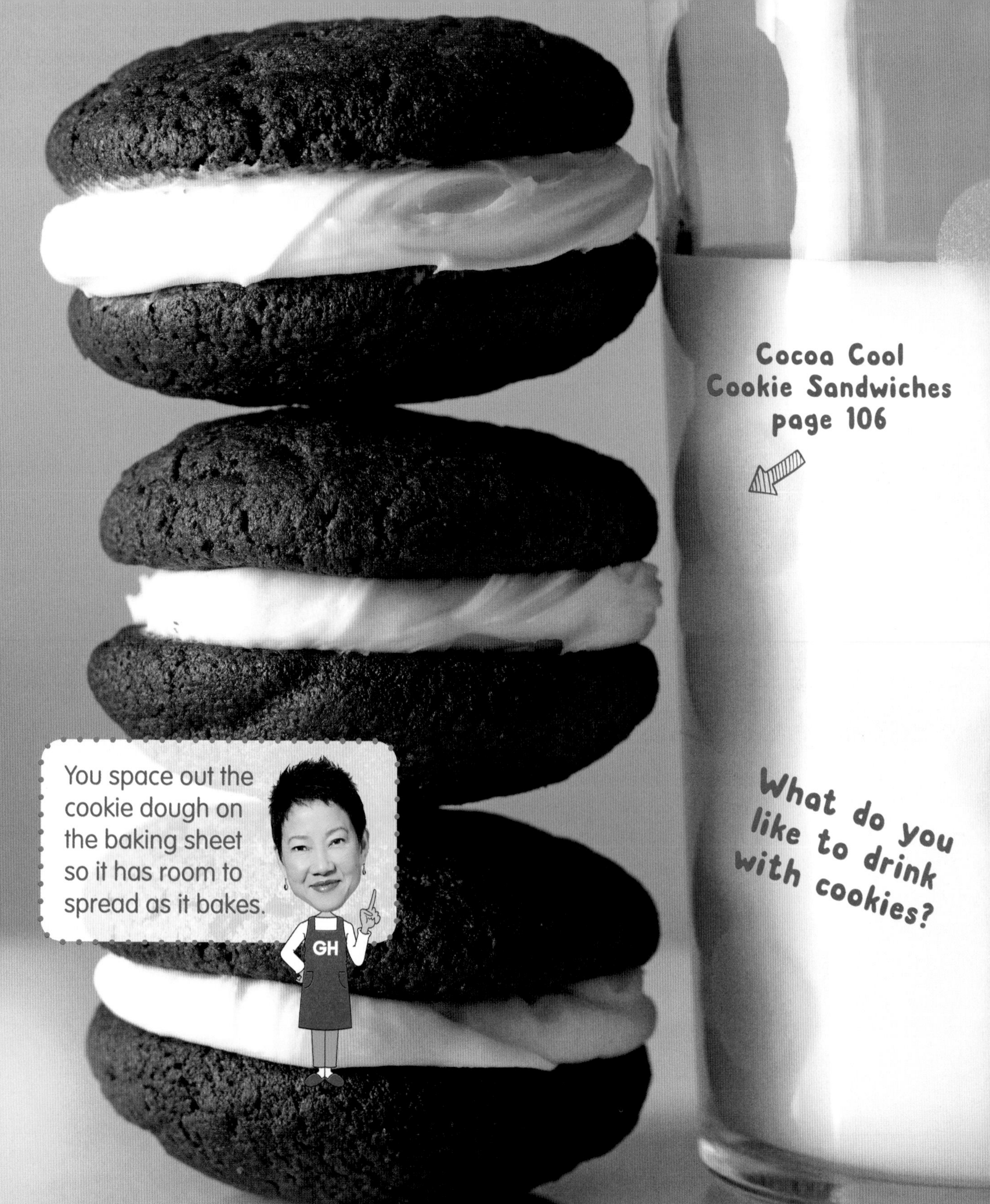
Cocoa Cool
Cookie Sandwiches
page 106
You space out the cookie dough on the baking sheet so it has room to spread as it bakes.
GH
What do you like to drink with cookies?

That's a Pizza Alright!

This dessert pizza has all of the elements of a regular pizza, just sweeter!

Cookie = pizza crust
Cream cheese mixture = sauce
Berries = pizza toppings

Berry Cool Cookie Pizza

Prepare Your Ingredients

All-purpose flour, for the parchment paper

1 16-ounce package refrigerated sugar cookie dough

2 tablespoons strawberry jam

2 tablespoons fresh lemon juice

1 pound strawberries, hulled and cut into pieces

1½ cups blueberries

1 8-ounce package cream cheese, at room temperature

¼ cup confectioners' sugar

2 cups refrigerated whipped topping

Serves 12

Ready to eat in 45 minutes

Gather Your Kitchen Tools

Parchment paper

Rolling pin

Ruler

Baking sheet

Oven mitts

Wire rack

Measuring cups and spoons

2 large bowls

Silicone spatula

Electric mixer

serrated knife

What other berries or fruit would you try on this pizza?

Make Your Berry Cool Cookie Pizza

1. Heat the oven to 350°F.

2. Sprinkle a little flour on a piece of parchment paper and spread it around. Shape the cookie dough into a disk, then roll it out on the parchment paper into a 12-inch-wide circle, following the directions on page 23. Slide the parchment paper (with the cookie dough) onto a baking sheet.

3. Bake until lightly golden brown, 15 to 18 minutes. Transfer the cookie (still on the parchment paper) to a wire rack and let it cool for at least 15 minutes.

4. While the cookie is baking and cooling, add the jam and the lemon juice to a large bowl and mix them together using a silicone spatula. Add the strawberries and blueberries and toss to coat. Set aside.

5. Add the cream cheese and confectioners' sugar to another large bowl. Using an electric mixer, beat the cream cheese and sugar until smooth, about 1 minute. Add the whipped topping and beat again until everything is just combined.

6. Spread the cream cheese mixture onto the cooled cookie, leaving a ½-inch border. Top with the berry mixture and slice into 12 wedges to serve.

Red Velvet Cookies

Prepare Your Ingredients

2 cups all-purpose flour

½ cup Dutch process cocoa powder

1 teaspoon baking soda

1 teaspoon kosher salt

1 cup (2 sticks) unsalted butter, at room temperature

¾ cup packed brown sugar

½ cup granulated sugar

1 large egg

1 teaspoon red gel paste food coloring

2 teaspoons pure vanilla extract

1 12-ounce package semisweet chocolate chips

Gather Your Kitchen Tools

2 baking sheets

Parchment paper

2 large bowls

Measuring cups and spoons

Whisk

Electric mixer

Silicone spatula

Oven mitts

Wire rack

Make Your Red Velvet Cookies

1. Heat the oven to 350°F. Line 2 baking sheets with parchment paper. In large bowl, whisk together flour, cocoa, baking soda and salt, following the directions on page 18. Set aside.

2. Using an electric mixer, beat together the butter, brown sugar and granulated sugar in another large bowl on medium speed until combined, about 3 minutes. Add the egg, food coloring and vanilla and mix until just combined.

3. Reduce the mixer speed to low and add the flour mixture, mixing until just combined. Fold in the chocolate chips.

4. Scoop heaping 2 tablespoonfuls of dough onto the prepared sheets, spacing them 1½ inches apart.

5. Bake, rotating the baking sheets halfway through, until the cookies are golden brown around the edges, 9 to 12 minutes total.

6. Let cool for 5 minutes on the pans, then slide the parchment (and cookies) onto a wire rack and let cool for at least 5 minutes more before serving.

Chocolate-Caramel Mug Cake

Prepare Your Ingredients

¼ cup all-purpose flour

2 tablespoons granulated sugar

2 tablespoons unsweetened cocoa powder

¼ teaspoon baking powder

⅛ teaspoon kosher salt

⅓ cup whole milk

2 tablespoons unsalted butter, melted

2 teaspoons pure vanilla extract

4 caramel squares, quartered

¼ cup toasted pecans, chopped

Serves 1

Ready to eat in 10 minutes

Gather Your Kitchen Tools

12-ounce mug

Fork

Silicone spatula

Why didn't the teddy bear finish his mug cake?
He was stuffed!
Ha!
Ha!
Ha!

Make Your Chocolate Mug Cake

1. In a mug, use a fork to whisk together the flour, sugar, cocoa powder, baking powder and salt. Carefully pour in the milk, butter and vanilla, following the directions on page 17. Mix together with a silicone spatula. Fold in the caramel and pecans.
2. Microwave on high for about 90 seconds, until just cooked through.

IMPORTANT!
Cool your cake for at least 5 minutes before digging in!

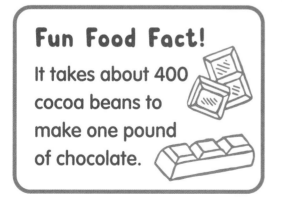

Fun Food Fact!
It takes about 400 cocoa beans to make one pound of chocolate.

Ice Cream Cake Pops

Prepare Your Ingredients

1 pint blueberries

1 quart vanilla ice cream, slightly softened

2 pints red raspberry sorbet, slightly softened

Star sprinkles (optional)

Makes 10 cake pops

Ready to eat in 8 hours, 15 minutes

Gather Your Kitchen Tools

10- by 5-inch loaf pan

Parchment paper

Electric mixer

2 large bowls

Silicone spatula

10 wooden craft sticks

Knife

You can use any fruits and flavors of ice cream and sorbet to make the Ice Cream Cake Pops of your dreams! We made ours for the Fourth of July.

Make Your Ice Cream Cake Pops

1. Line a loaf pan with parchment paper, leaving a 2-inch overhang on all four sides. Scatter the blueberries evenly into the pan.

2. Using an electric mixer, beat the ice cream in a large bowl on medium speed just until smooth. Use a silicone spatula to spread the ice cream on top of the blueberries and place the pan in the freezer until firm.

3. In a second large bowl, beat the sorbet with the electric mixer until just smooth. Remove the pan from the freezer, and use a silicone spatula to spread the sorbet on top of the ice cream layer. Top with sprinkles, if using.

4. Push the craft sticks into the loaf, spacing them 1 inch apart down the center of the loaf and three-quarters of the way to the bottom of the pan. Freeze until firm, at least 8 hours.

5. When ready to serve, use the overhangs to remove the ice cream from the pan. Peel away the parchment paper and carefully cut between the craft sticks to make ten pops.

What did the galaxy say when it made a mistake?
I'm star-ry!

Ice Cream
Cake Pops
page 116

Choco-Striped
Pretzels
page 120

Choco-Striped Pretzels

Prepare Your Ingredients

8 ounces dark, milk or white chocolate chips or strawberry candy melts, or a combination

10 small pretzels

Serves 10

Ready to eat in 25 minutes

That's some hot chocolate! Use a fork if you want to dip your pretzel all the way into the melted chocolate.

Gather Your Kitchen Tools

Baking sheet

Parchment paper

Small bowls

Silicone spatula

Why are these Choco-Striped Pretzels never on time?

They're made with chocoLATE!

Make Your Choco-Striped Pretzels

1. Line a baking sheet with parchment paper. Set aside.
2. Place one of the types of candy in a small bowl. Microwave on high, stirring with a silicone spatula every 20 seconds, until melted. (This should take about a minute.)
3. Dip each pretzel fully or halfway into the melted candy. Let any extra candy drip off the pretzel, or tap it on the side of the bowl to shake off the extra. Place the candy-dipped pretzels onto the prepared baking sheet and let the candy set.
4. If you are using a second type of candy, melt it in the microwave following the instructions in step 2.
5. Using a silicone spatula, drizzle the pretzels with the second candy, or the same candy, and let set before serving, about 15 minutes.

Another Nom

Make Choco-Dipped Clementines! Melt 4 ounces bittersweet chocolate and dip half of each clementine segment to coat. Place on a parchment paper-lined baking sheet and sprinkle each segment with a pinch of coarse sea salt. Try the same technique with apple slices, pear slices, grapes, animal crackers or even potato chips! Yum!

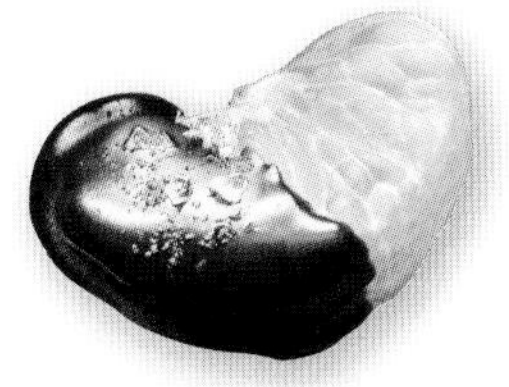

page 124

page 128

Yum! Yum!

page 130

page 134

page 136

page 138

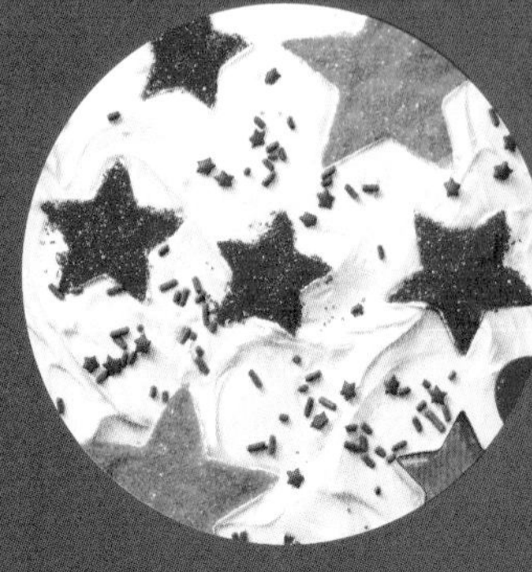
page 140

page 144

YUM!

page 146

page 150

page 152

page 156

- Chapter 6 -
Fun Foods & Holidays Treats

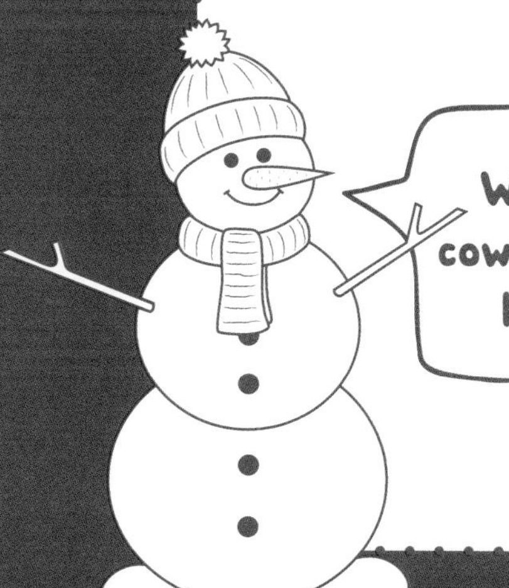

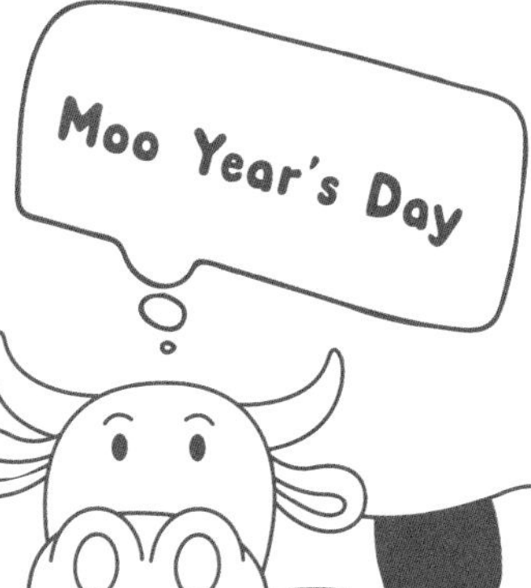

Halloween!

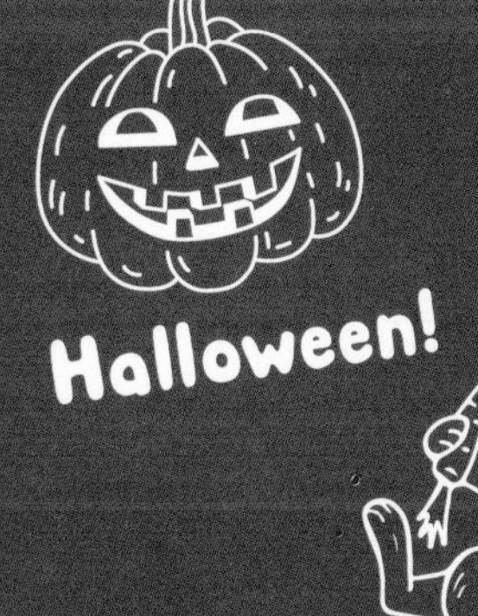

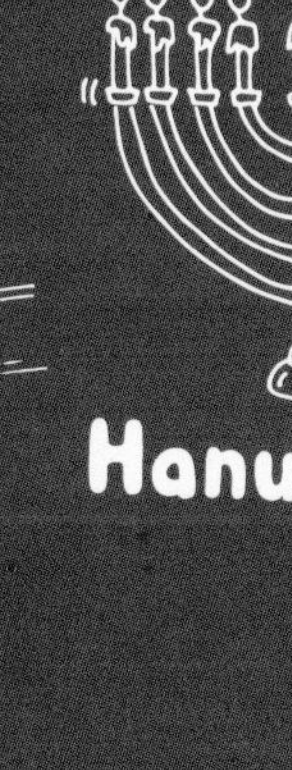

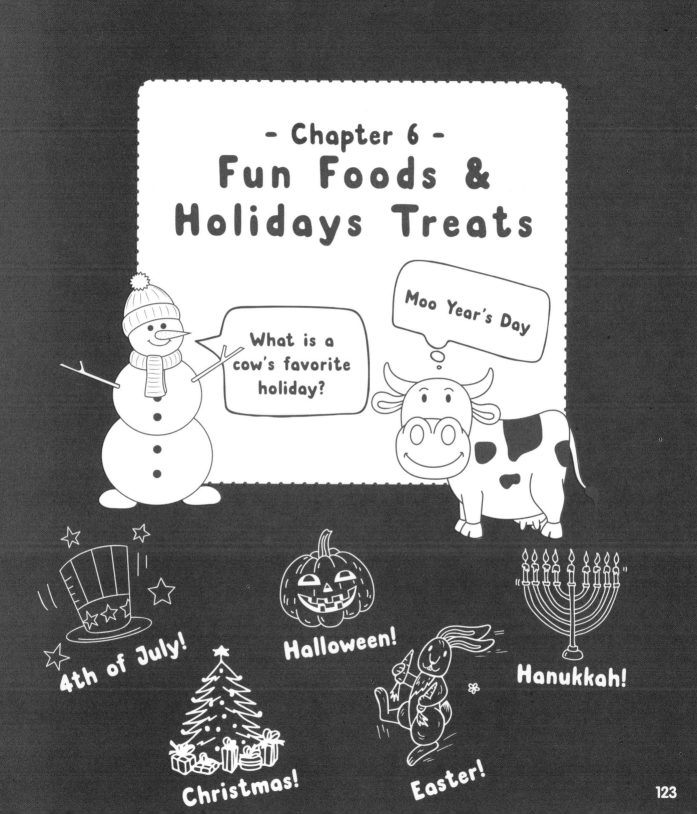

Jell-O Oceans

Prepare Your Ingredients

1 6-ounce package blue Jell-O

Gummy fish candy

Your choice of:

- Teddy Grahams
- Gummy ring candy
- Green fruit slice gummy candy
- Pretzel sticks
- Sour strap gummy candy
- Gummy triangle candy

Serves 8

Ready to eat in 4 hours or until firm to the touch

Gather Your Kitchen Tools

Measuring cups

8 small clear cups

Toothpicks

Resealable plastic sandwich bag

Cutting board

Fork

Kids' safety scissors

What do you call a bear who got caught in the rain?
A drizzly bear!
HA HA HA HA HA HA

Make Your Jell-O Oceans

1. Make liquid blue gelatin according to the package directions. Pour into small cups and follow the package directions to set.

2. When the Jell-O is firm, push a few gummy fish into each cup using a toothpick. Decorate the tops with snacks and candy to create your own beach scenes. Surfs up!

   - **To make a sandy beach:** Put a few Teddy Grahams in a sandwich bag—make sure the top is zipped! Lay the bag on a cutting board, then use a fork to crush the grahams while they're still in the bag. Press and press until the crumbs look like sand, then sprinkle them over one side of the Jell-O to make your own little beach!
   - **To make a Teddy swimmer in a floaty:** Place a Teddy Graham inside a gummy ring, then gently press it into the Jell-O water.
   - **To make a palm tree:** Stick a green fruit slice gummy on top of a pretzel stick, then stick it in the crushed graham cracker sand.
   - **To make a beach towel:** Using scissors, cut a sour strap gummy into little rectangular strips, then place on your beach.
   - **To make a sailboat:** Take one fruit slice gummy and one triangle gummy and stick them on a toothpick. Stick the boat on the Jell-O water.

Check out the photo on the next page for decorating ideas!

Jell-O Oceans
page 124
Fruit slice sailboat
(use a toothpick
to secure!)
Teddy swimmer
in a floaty
Crushed
cookie
beach
Pretzel stick &
green fruit
slice palm trees
Sour strap
beach towel
Gummy
fish
Looking at the photo will help you figure out how you want to decorate your Jell-O Oceans. Sometimes a picture can be just as helpful as the written directions.
GH

A Rainbow That Really Pop(corn)s! Plus Cutest-Thing-Ever Popcorn Sheep page 128
Why did the pilot fly through the rainbow during her flight test?
So she'd pass with flying colors!

A Rainbow That Really Pop(corn)s! Plus Cutest-Thing-Ever Popcorn Sheep

Prepare Your Ingredients

Rainbow

2 ounces blue candy melts

2 ounces purple candy melts

4 ounces green candy melts

4 ounces yellow candy melts

6 ounces orange candy melts

6 ounces red candy melts

3½ cups air-popped popcorn, tossed with a pinch of kosher salt

Clouds and Sheep

12 ounces white chocolate chips

2 cups air-popped popcorn, tossed with a pinch of kosher salt

Black fondant

Candy eyes

Gather Your Kitchen Tools

Baking sheet

Parchment paper

Bowl

Pencil

6 medium bowls

Silicone spatula

Measuring cups

Large bowl

Make the Rainbow

1. Line a baking sheet with parchment paper. Use a bowl or saucepan lid to trace half a circle onto the parchment paper.

2. Place each color candy melt into separate bowls. Working with one color at time and starting with the blue, microwave the candy melts on high for 20 seconds and stir with a silicone spatula. Repeat, heating and stirring until melted and smooth.

3. Fold ¼ cup popcorn into the blue candy melts until fully coated. Using the traced arch as a guide, squish and shape the popcorn in a single layer into one stripe of the rainbow. Repeat with the remaining candy melts and popcorn using:
   - ¼ cup popcorn for purple
   - ½ cup popcorn for green
   - ½ cup popcorn for yellow
   - 1 cup popcorn for orange
   - 1 cup popcorn for red

Make the Cloud and Sheep

1. Melt the white chocolate in a large bowl in 30-second intervals, stirring between each with a silicone spatula, until smooth. Fold the popcorn into the chocolate until fully coated. Pile some into a ball at one end of the rainbow. You've got a cloud!

2. Now make three piles of varying shapes with the remaining popcorn. Use your hands to shape the fondant into super-cute sheep faces and ears and stick onto the popcorn while it's still tacky. Then use a small dab of water to stick on the eyes.

3. Let set before serving, at least 15 minutes.

Really Lucky Shamrock Cupcakes

Prepare Your Ingredients

Makes 12 cupcakes

Ready to eat in 1 hour

Cupcakes

Nonstick cooking spray, for the pan

1½ cups all-purpose flour

1½ teaspoons baking powder

¼ teaspoon kosher salt

¾ cup granulated sugar

½ cup (1 stick) unsalted butter, at room temperature

2 large eggs

½ teaspoon vanilla extract

¾ cup whole milk

Decoration

1 to 1½ cups vanilla frosting

Green sanding sugar

Pretzel sticks

Sour candy straps (optional)

Yellow nonpareils (optional)

Gather Your Kitchen Tools

Mini muffin pan

Mini cupcake liners

Medium bowl

Measuring cups and spoons

Whisk

3 large bowls

Electric mixer

Silicone spatula

Aluminum foil

Oven mitts

Wire rack

Offset spatula or butter knife

Make the Cupcakes

1. Heat the oven to 350°F and oil a mini muffin pan, following the directions on page 22. Place mini cupcake liners in each cup.

2. In a medium bowl, whisk together the flour, baking powder and salt, following the directions on page 18. Set aside.

3. Using an electric mixer, beat the sugar and butter in a large bowl on medium-high speed until light and fluffy, about 3 minutes. Reduce the mixer speed to medium and add the eggs, one at a time, beating to mix each one in before adding the next. Beat in the vanilla, scraping down the sides of the bowl as needed.

4. Reduce the mixer speed to low and add the flour mixture and then the milk in the following pattern: one third flour—half milk—one third flour—last half milk—last third flour.

5. Beat until the batter is just mixed. (Try not to mix too much or the cupcakes will be tough instead of fluffy!)

6. Divide the batter between the muffin cups, pouring about 1½ tablespoons into each cup.

7. Ball up a little piece of foil and stick it between the outside of each liner and the pan to create an indent. Then place 2 small rectangles of foil (3 sheets thick) on opposite sides of the liners to create small hearts.

8. Bake until golden brown, about 12 to 18 minutes. Remove from the oven and place on a wire rack to cool completely. See the next page for tips on decorating.

Really Lucky Shamrock Cupcakes page 130

Make Cupcakes that Shamrock!

Now create the shamrock cupcakes by frosting the indented mini cupcakes with the buttercream frosting and dipping them in green sanding sugar. Then, arrange three cupcakes so the pointed sides touch to create the shamrocks. Use a ½-inch piece of pretzel for each stem. Frost mini cupcakes and dip in yellow nonpareils to make dandelions!

Animal
Crackers
page 134

Animal Crackers

Prepare Your Ingredients

Cream cheese, at room temperature

Large round crackers

Mini round crackers

Almonds, whole and sliced

Cashews, whole and sliced

Cheese, sliced

Golden and regular raisins

Dried cranberries

Fresh currants (or raisins or cranberries, chopped)

Chives

Cucumbers, sliced into rings

Carrots, sliced into ear shapes and cut into noses

Red bell pepper, cut into triangles

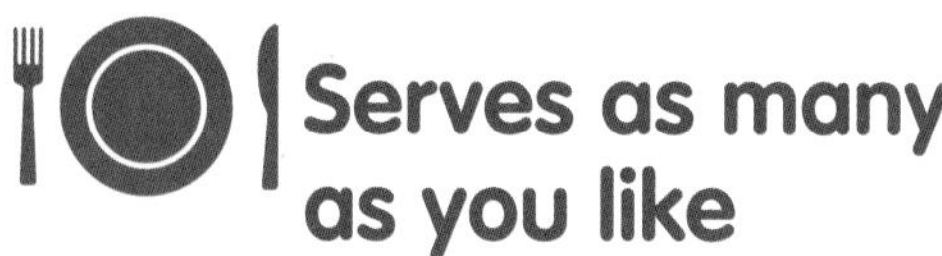

Serves as many as you like

Ready to eat in 20 minutes

Gather Your Kitchen Tools

Butter knife or silicone spatula, for spreading

What animal faces do you want to make?

Make Your Animal Crackers

Spread cream cheese on the large round crackers, then press on the other ingredients to make funny, "furry" faces. Create any animal faces you like, or try out the creatures you see here! We made:

- **A hedgehog** with almond spikes, currant eyes and a raisin nose.
- **An owl** with almond ears, cucumber and currant eyes, a cashew beak and almond feathers.
- **A racoon bandit** with almond ears, currant eyes, a cheese burglar's mask and a raisin nose.
- **A fox** with red bell pepper ears, carrot and currant eyes and a raisin nose.
- **A bunny** with purple carrot ears, raisin eyes, a carrot nose and mini cracker cheeks.
- **A silly dog** with almond ears, mini cracker and currant eyes, chive whiskers, a cranberry nose and a sliced carrot tongue.

Why shouldn't you cross a turtle and a porcupine?
Because you get a slow poke!

Lobste-llar Cookies

Prepare Your Ingredients

Red-and-white cherry ring candy

Uncooked spaghetti, broken into pieces

Gummy cherry fruit slice candy

Gummy orange fruit slice candy

Light corn syrup

Candy eyes

Round shortbread cookies

Makes as many as you like

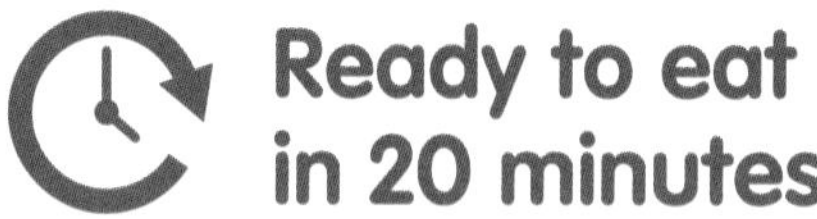
Ready to eat in 20 minutes

Gather Your Kitchen Tools

Butter knife or kid's safety knife

Toothpicks (optional)

Bend the gummies to make the lobsters look like they are swimming!

IMPORTANT!
Be sure to remove the uncooked spaghetti or toothpicks before chowing down on these lobsters!

Make Your Lobste-llar Cookies

1. Cut a cherry ring in half, and then cut a notch in one end to make claws. Attach them with uncooked spaghetti or toothpicks (remove before eating) to a gummy cherry slice body.

2. Cut a piece of gummy orange slice for the tail and stick the cut side to the cherry slice body. It might stick on its own, but if it doesn't use a drop of water to make it sticky.

3. Use a dab of corn syrup to glue on candy eyes and let dry. Place the lobsters on shortbread cookie islands.

Cookie Garden

Prepare Your Ingredients

Licorice twists in different colors

Green licorice twists

Chocolate wafer cookies

Light corn syrup

Makes as many as you like

Ready to eat in 15 minutes

Gather Your Kitchen Tools

Butter knife or kid's safety knife

Toothpick

What did the baker get when she messed up her wafer recipe?
Cookie-doh!

Make Your Cookie Garden

1. To make the flowers, cut colored licorice twists into ¾-inch pieces.
2. To make the stems, cut green licorice twists into 1-inch pieces, then cut each half into thin slices.
3. Arrange different color flowers on the cookies. When you like how it looks, use a toothpick dipped in light corn syrup to glue each petal and stem to the cookies. Spring has never looked sweeter!

Your licorice pieces will look like petals!

Star-Studded Sparkle Cake

Prepare Your Ingredients

Serves 12

Ready to eat in 1 hour, 30 minutes

Cake

1 cup (2 sticks) unsalted butter, at room temperature, plus more for the pan

3 cups all-purpose flour

1 tablespoon baking powder

1 teaspoon kosher salt

1¾ cup granulated sugar

4 large eggs

2 teaspoons pure vanilla extract

1¼ cups whole milk, at room temperature

Decoration

2 cups vanilla frosting

Red sanding sugar

Blue sanding sugar

Turn to page 142 for how to decorate your cake!

Gather Your Kitchen Tools

9- by 13-inch cake pan

Parchment paper

3 large bowls

Measuring cups and spoons

Whisk

Electric mixer

Silicone spatula

Oven mitts

Wooden pick

Wire rack

Star-shaped cookie cutters

Make the Star-Studded Sparkle Cake

1. Heat the oven to 325°F. Butter a 9- by 13-inch cake pan and line the bottom with parchment paper, leaving a 2-inch overhang on the two long sides. Butter the parchment paper.

2. In a large bowl, whisk together the flour, baking powder and salt, following the directions on page 18. Set aside.

3. In another large bowl, combine the butter and granulated sugar. Using an electric mixer, beat on low speed until well mixed. Increase the speed to medium-high and beat until light and fluffy, about 3 minutes.

4. Reduce the mixer speed to medium and add the eggs, one at a time, beating until each is lightly mixed in before adding the next egg. Then mix in the vanilla.

5. Reduce the mixer speed to low and add the flour mixture and milk in the following pattern: one third flour—half milk—one third flour—last half milk—last third flour.

6. Beat until the batter is just mixed. (Try not to mix too much or the cake will be flat instead of fluffy!)

7. Spread the batter into the prepared pan. Bake until a wooden pick inserted in the center comes out clean, about 40 minutes. Let the cake cool in the pan for 10 minutes, then, using overhangs, remove from the pan to a wire rack. Let cool completely.

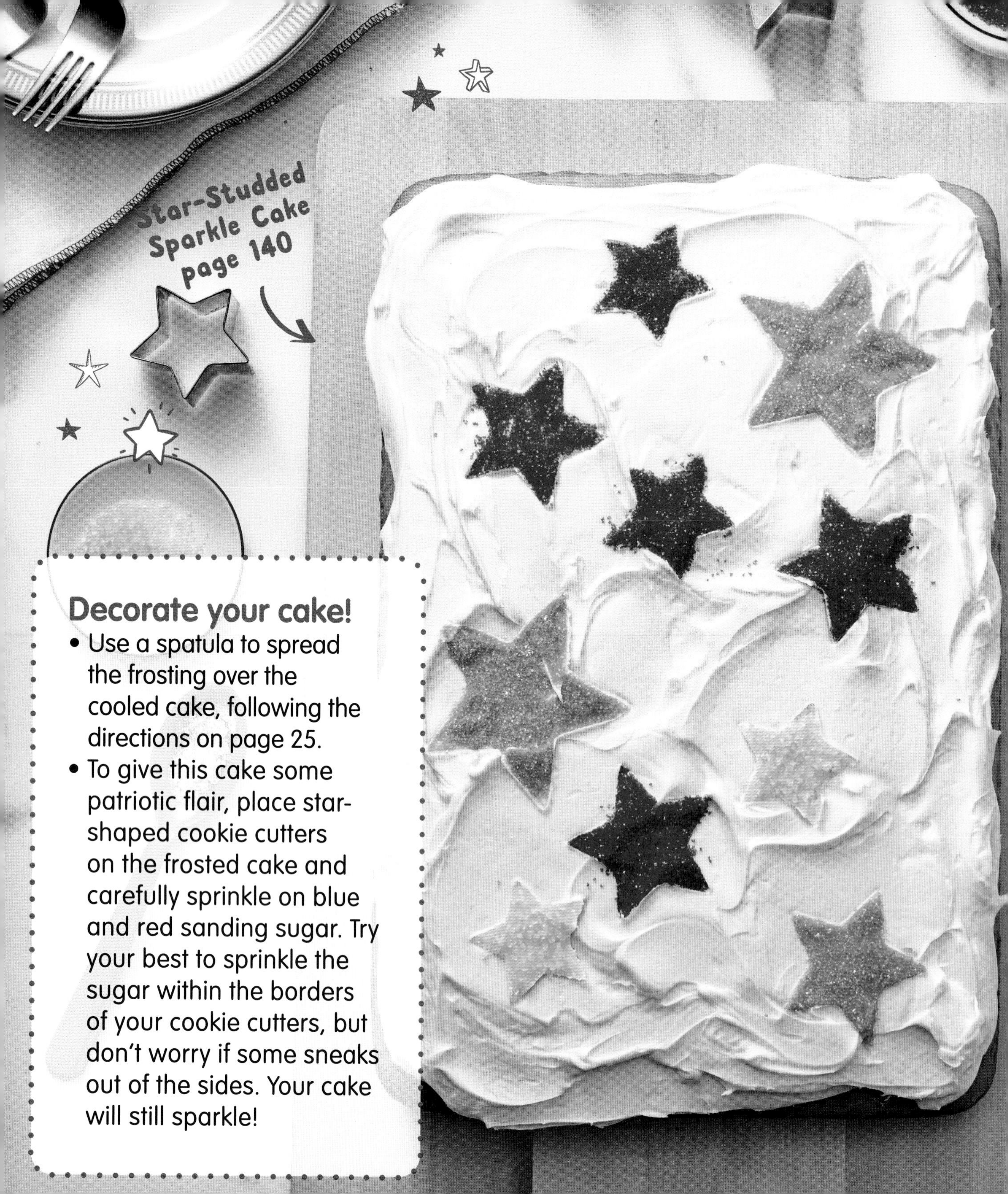

Decorate your cake!

- Use a spatula to spread the frosting over the cooled cake, following the directions on page 25.
- To give this cake some patriotic flair, place star-shaped cookie cutters on the frosted cake and carefully sprinkle on blue and red sanding sugar. Try your best to sprinkle the sugar within the borders of your cookie cutters, but don't worry if some sneaks out of the sides. Your cake will still sparkle!

Here Comes Peter Cottontail Cookies page 144
What game do rabbits like best?
Hopscotch!

Here Comes Peter Cottontail Cookies

Prepare Your Ingredients

1 16-ounce package refrigerated sugar cookie dough

All-purpose flour, for dusting

Pink frosting

White frosting

Mini marshmallows

Pink M&M's

Pink candy-coated sunflower seeds

Makes about 12 cookies

Ready to eat in 2 hours, 30 minutes

Gather Your Kitchen Tools

2 baking sheets

Parchment paper

Rolling pin

3-inch round cookie cutter

1-inch egg-shaped cookie cutter

Pancake turner

Oven mitts

Wire rack

Silicone spatula

Make Your Here Comes Peter Cottontail Cookies

1. Heat the oven to the temperature on the cookie dough package. Line 2 baking sheets with parchment paper, following the directions on page 21.

2. Sprinkle flour over your work surface and the rolling pin to prevent the dough from sticking. Roll out the cookie dough until it's about ⅛ inch thick, following the directions on page 23. Coat the 3-inch round cutter in flour and then cut rounds from the dough for bunny bodies. Use a pancake turner to transfer the bunny bodies to one of the baking sheets.

3. Dip the 1-inch egg-shaped cookie cutter in flour and cut ovals for feet. You'll need 2 feet for each body. Place the feet on the other baking sheet.

4. Bake as directed on cookie dough package, checking on the feet at the halfway mark (they are smaller so they will cook faster!). Transfer the cookies to a wire rack and let them cool completely.

5. Study the photo on the previous spread to see how to put together the bunny butts and feet. First, use a spatula to spread white or pink frosting in the centers of the cooled cookie rounds and ovals to match the photo. See page 25 for directions on how to spread frosting.

6. Before the frosting dries, press 2 oval cookies into the edges of each round for feet. Then press a mini marshmallow into the center of each butt for the tail. Place pink M&M's in the middle of the feet and pink candy-coated sunflower seeds on the edges of the feet for toes. Let your bunny butts rest at room temperature until the frosting is set, about 2 hours.

Bud the Beaver Pancakes

Prepare Your Ingredients

1 large very ripe banana

2 cups pancake mix, plus the ingredients to make it

¼ cup creamy peanut butter or other nut butter

1 teaspoon pure vanilla extract

Pure maple syrup, melted chocolate, banana slices, blueberries and white Cheddar, for decorating

Serves 4

Ready to eat in 15 minutes

Gather Your Kitchen Tools

2 medium bowls

Fork

Measuring cups and spoons

Silicone spatula

Griddle or large nonstick pan

Pancake turner

What snack did the beaver serve at the party?
Wood chips!
HA HA HA
HA HA HA

Make Your Bud the Beaver Pancakes

1. In a medium bowl, use a fork to mash the banana with whatever liquid or eggs the pancake mix calls for. Use a silicone spatula to mix in the peanut butter and vanilla, then set it aside.

2. Dump the pancake mix into another medium bowl. Use a silicone spatula to stir in the banana mixture until just blended.

3. Cook the pancakes as directed on the packaging, making pancakes of different sizes and shapes to create a beaver. (See the picture on the next page for ideas!)

4. Assemble the pancakes to resemble a beaver. Use maple syrup, melted chocolate, banana slices, blueberries and cheese to create a face and a tail.

Fun Food Fact!

The average sugar maple tree produces anywhere from 5 to 15 gallons of sap, which means the sap from 2½ trees needs to be combined to make a single gallon of syrup. Then the sap is cooked down to make syrup. It takes sap from 2½ trees to make 1 gallon of syrup!

Bud the Beaver Pancakes page 146
Bud will be your new best friend at breakfast!

Boo-scotti
page 150

Boo-scotti

Prepare Your Ingredients

1 cup white chocolate chips

4 biscotti

3 tablespoons dark chocolate chips

Makes 4 cookies

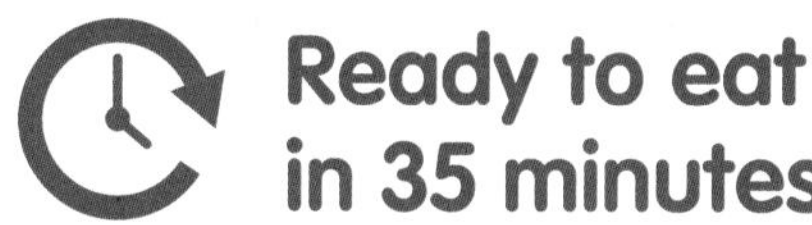

Ready to eat in 35 minutes

Gather Your Kitchen Tools

Baking sheet

Parchment paper

Small cup

Silicone spatula

Small bowl

Toothpick

Biscotti are a special kind of Italian cookie—they are **baked twice**, which makes them super crunchy. They're perfect for dunking in milk or hot chocolate!

What's a ghost's favorite fruit?

Boo-berries!
Ha!
Ha!
Ha!

Make Your Boo-scotti

1. Line a baking sheet with parchment paper.
2. In a cup, microwave the white chocolate on high, stirring with a silicone spatula every 20 seconds until melted. Use a dry kitchen towel to handle the cup—it might get hot!
3. Dip the biscotti into the melted white chocolate, then place on the parchment paper–lined baking sheet. Refrigerate for about 15 minutes, until the chocolate is set (no longer sticky).
4. In a small bowl, microwave the dark chocolate until melted. This should take only a few seconds.
5. Take the biscotti out of the fridge. Dip a toothpick into the dark chocolate and use it to draw faces on the cookies. Make spooky faces, silly faces, happy faces—whatever you like! Put the boo-scotti back in the fridge until the faces are set, about 10 minutes.

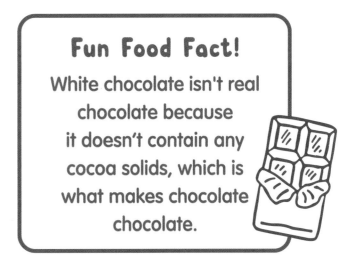

Fun Food Fact!

White chocolate isn't real chocolate because it doesn't contain any cocoa solids, which is what makes chocolate chocolate.

Sugar Cookie Trees

Prepare Your Ingredients

2¾ cups all-purpose flour

½ teaspoon baking powder

¼ teaspoon kosher salt

1 cup (2 sticks) unsalted butter, at room temperature

¾ cup granulated sugar

1 large egg

1½ teaspoons pure vanilla extract

Green gel food coloring

Royal icing

Confectioners' sugar, for dusting (optional)

Make the dough a little darker than you want it to be. The cookies will be a lighter color once they are baked.

Makes 24 cookies

Ready to eat in 45 minutes

Gather Your Kitchen Tools

2 large bowls

Measuring cups and spoons

Whisk

Electric mixer

Silicone spatula

Plastic wrap

Rolling pin

Parchment paper

2 baking sheets

Graduated round cookie cutters

Small star-shaped cookie cutter

Oven mitts

Pancake turner

Wire racks

Make the Dough

1. In a large bowl, whisk together the flour, baking powder and salt, following the directions on page 18. Set aside.

2. In another large bowl, add the butter and granulated sugar. Using an electric mixer, beat on high speed until light and fluffy, about 3 minutes. Beat in the egg and then the vanilla.

3. Reduce the mixer speed to low and add the flour mixture, a little at a time. Beat until just combined. Divide the dough into four equal parts, and place one part back in the mixing bowl. Shape each of the three other parts into a loose ball and wrap it in plastic wrap. Set the wrapped dough balls aside.

4. Add 2–3 drops of green food coloring to the dough in the bowl and mix until it is evenly green.

5. Lay out a sheet of parchment paper and place the green dough on it. Place a second piece of parchment paper on top of the dough and roll the dough into a circle that is ⅛-inch thick, following the directions on page 23. Chill the dough in the refrigerator for 30 minutes or freezer for 15 minutes.

6. Repeat steps 4 and 5 with two other dough balls. If you want, add different amounts of food coloring to make a couple shades of green.

7. Take the last dough ball and divide it in half. Place one half in the mixing bowl and follow steps 4 and 5 to color and roll it out. Then roll the uncolored ball of dough between two sheets of parchment paper and chill.

Turn the page to learn how to make the cookies

Make the Cookies

1. Heat the oven to 350°F. Line 2 baking sheets with parchment paper. Remove one of the green dough circles from the refrigerator. Take four different sizes of round cookie cutters, dip them in flour and cut out the cookies. Place the cookies onto the prepared baking sheets, making sure to put the smaller cookies on a different sheet than the bigger cookies. Squeeze the dough scraps together into a ball, roll it between two pieces of parchment paper, chill and cut more cookies. Repeat with the rest of the green chilled dough, cutting an equal amount of each of the sizes. Finally, cut the uncolored dough into star cookies and add them to the baking sheet with the smaller cookies.

2. Bake the cookies, rotating the baking sheets after 5 minutes, until the cookies are light golden brown around the edges, 10 to 12 minutes. (Make sure to check on the stars after 8 to 9 minutes. They are smaller cookies and will bake faster. Take them out when they are golden brown.) Let the cookies cool for 5 minutes before moving them to wire racks to cool completely.

Assemble the Cookies

1. To build the trees, use an offset spatula to spread a thin layer of royal icing on one large cookie, then place a second large cookie of a different green on top. Repeat with the next smaller size cookie until you've stacked two of each size to make the tree.

2. Dip the bottom two points of a star cookie in the icing and add it to the top of the tree. Dust with confectioners' sugar "snow" if you'd like.

Why did the big pine tree yell at the little pine tree?
Because it was very knotty.
Alternate light green and dark green cookies when stacking your trees!

PB and Fudge Dizzy Dreidels

Prepare Your Ingredients

8 ounces peanut butter fudge

10 thin pretzel sticks

¾ cup milk chocolate chips

¼ cup white chocolate chips

10 Hershey's Kisses

Makes 10 dreidels

Ready to eat in 30 minutes

Gather Your Kitchen Tools

Baking sheet

Parchment paper

Knife

Cutting board

Measuring cups

2 small bowls

Silicone spatula

Resealable plastic sandwich bag

Scissors

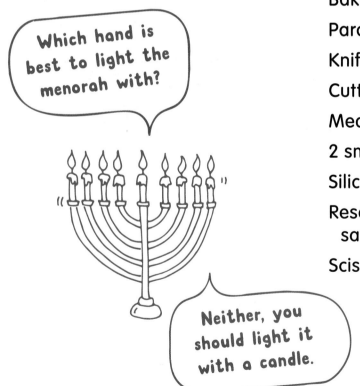

Which hand is best to light the menorah with?

Neither, you should light it with a candle.

Make Your Dizzy Dreidels

1. Line a baking sheet with parchment paper.

2. Cut the peanut butter fudge into 1-inch by 1-inch cubes. Push a pretzel stick into one side of each cube.

3. In a small bowl, microwave the milk chocolate chips on high, stirring with a silicone spatula every 20 seconds, until melted.

4. Use a dab of melted chocolate to stick a Hershey's Kiss on the opposite side of each cube, creating a dreidel shape.

5. Hold the pretzel, dip the dreidel into the melted milk chocolate and let the extra chocolate drip off before placing the dreidels onto the prepared baking sheet. Refrigerate until the chocolate is set, at least 15 minutes.

6. Melt white chocolate chips as in step 3. Place melted white chocolate into a resealable plastic bag, snip off one corner and pipe on Hebrew letters.

Index

IMAGE CREDITS

Top - UP, Center - CTR, Bottom - LO, Left - LE, Right - RT, Background - BG

Cover: Evi Abeler FRONT, Danielle Daly FLAP UP RT, Mike Garten BACK LE/BACK RT/FLAP UP LE/FLAP CTR RT/FLAP LO, Steve Giralt FLAP CTR LE, ©Johnny Miller BACK CTR, Kat Teutsch BACK LO, ©Barrirret/Adobe Stock BACK CTR, ©Boxerx/Adobe Stock BACK CTR/LO LE/ LO RT, ©Mhatzapa/Adobe Stock SPINE/BACK CTR RT/BACK LO LE/BACK LO RT, ©Farah Sadikhova/Shutterstock UP RT

Endpapers: Shutterstock ©Tupungato

Our Test Kitchen: Mike Garten (6, 8 CTR LE, 9 UP LE/LO LE, 11 LO RT, 16 LO RT, 28, 34, 38, 63, 65, 77, 93, 103, 108, 116, 126, 150, 152); Chris Eckert (8 LO RT, 32 LO RT, 70); NXM Photo (9 CTR RT, 40, 80, 120); Sam MacAvoy (10 LO LE, 36, 47, 95, 139); Patrick MacLeod (10 UP LE, 84, 136) Ari Michelson (11 UP RT, 56, 101, 148)

Photography: Mike Garten (2, 26, 30, 31, 34, 38, 39, 41, 44, 45, 49, 50, 52, 71, 75, 78, 82, 83, 88, 94, 95, 96, 98, 99, 102, 112, 115, 118, 119, 122, 127, 132, 137, 142, 143, 149, 155); ©Johnny Miller (4, 52, 59, 65); Danielle Daly (17, 18, 19, 20, 21, 22, 23, 24, 25, 52, 55, 70, 78, 83, 122, 126); ©Hector Sanchez (52, 58); ©Con Poulos (52,64, 96, 103); ©Steve Giralt (78, 89, 121, 122, 133, 134, 157); ©Romulo Yanes (96, 102); ©Kat Teutsch (96, 109); ©Linda Xiao (121); Erika Lapresto (122, 139); Evi Abeler (122, 148)

Adobe Stock: ©Barrirret (2, 52 UP, 78, 96, 122); ©DiBronzino (speech bubbles throughout); ©ahmad (arrows, 4, 29, 34, 35, 38, 41, 45, 47, 70, 71, 82, 83, 87, 88, 89, 93, 101, 102, 108, 127, 132, 139,142); ©Арина Уляшева (4); ©oxinoxi (parent warning icon throughout); ©Boxerx (arrows, 8, 9, 10, 13, 14, 15, 16, 19, 23, 25, 30, 31, 33, 39, 41, 44, 47, 49, 50, 58, 59, 61, 63, 64, 65, 75, 77, 95, 98, 99, 103, 109, 118, 125, 126, 133, 134, 140, 143, 148, 149, 153, 155); ©Gwens graphic studio (26 UP, 52 CTR); ©Anatoliy (26 LO, 52 LO); ©Fandorina Liza (27 CTR LE); © MoonBandit (27 CTR); ©Shamanistik_art (27 LO RT); ©Tofutyklein (27 LO CTR); ©Visual Generation (27 LO LE); ©Wonder-studio (27 CTR RT); ©Mark Stock (time icon 28, 32, 34, 35, 40, 42, 46, 48, 54, 56, 60, 62, 66, 68, 72, 75, 80, 84, 86, 90, 92 94, 98, 100, 104, 106, 110, 112, 114, 116, 120, 124, 128, 130, 134, 136, 138 140 144, 146, 150, 152, 156); ©martialred (place setting icon 28, 32, 34, 35, 40, 42, 46, 48, 54, 56, 60, 62, 66, 68, 72, 75, 80, 84, 86, 90, 92 94, 98, 100, 104, 106, 110, 112, 114, 116, 120, 124, 128, 130, 134, 136, 138 140 144, 146, 150, 152, 156); ©SmashingStocks (28); ©Елена Дрожжина (29 LO RT); ©Mhatzapa (29UP RT, 32 LO LE, 33 UP, 35 UP, 36, 38, 47, 95, 114 LO LE); ©Olha (30); ©HitToon.com (31); ©Aliaksandr Siamko (33 CTR);Tosca Digital (33 LO); ©psartstudio (35); ©lineartestpilot (35 LO, 63, 85, 132 CTR); ©Setory (37); ©Strichfiguren.de (ha ha illo 42, 53, 54, 82, 85, 92, 99, 104, 124, 146); ©francissmth (42); ©Елена Кутузова (45); ©tulpahn (49, 73, 75); ©scoutori (50); ©Ah_Leah (51); ©John Takai (53 LO LE); ©Josepperianes (53 UP RT/ UPLE); ©kronalux (53 CTR); ©Lida (53 CTR LE/CTR RT); ©Olllikeballoon (54, 60, 82, 104 LO LE, 138 CTR); ©uavector (58); ©Devitaayu (61, 120); ©Yulia Buchatskaya (62); ©jenny on the moon (66, 67); ©jivopira (70); ©Mictoon (71); ©JungleOutThere (72); ©Teploleta (79 LO LE); ©Evgenii Dolzhenkov (79 LO LE); ©mikailain (79 CTR); ©Siberian Art (79 LO CTR); ©Sybirko (79 UP RT); ©Claire Williams Art (80 LO LE); ©wanchana (80); ©_aine_ (87, 150); ©Astri (91 LE); ©dule964 (91 CTR, 114 LO RT); ©Lemonade Serenade (91 RT2); © Ирина Самойлова (91 UP); ©Olena (91 RT1); ©helen_f (92, 93, 138 RT); ©schakty (94, 109, 110); ©Anntre (97 LO CTR); ©Barysevich Lryna (97 CTR RT); ©corythoman (97 CTR LE, 123, 135 LE); ©padmasanjaya (97 LO RT); ©Veekicl (97 LO LE, 116 LO LE); ©fiodarpiatrykin (98); ©neapneap (99); ©topvectors (100, 104 LO RT); ©Mochipet (101); ©vitalka_ka (115, 151); ©Rawpixel.com (116, 117, 118); ©Symkin (117 LO LE); ©AllNikArt (123 LO RT, 142, 143 BG, 144); ©Decobrush (123 CTR LE); ©Irina (123 LO LE); ©Jehsomwang (123 UP RT); ©Natashapankina (123 CTR RT, 156, 157, 130, 131, 132 BG); ©Tatiana Luna (123 UP LE); ©Igor Zakowski (124 LO); ©Kebon Doodle (124 UP, 129); ©sararoom (135 RT); ©Olesia (137 LE); ©Надежда Аксенова (137 LE); ©Vectors Point (138 LE); ©Matias (140, 141, 142); ©dashtik (143 LO RT); ©MicroOne (146); ©Séa (147); ©Татьяна Петрова (155) **Getty Images:** ©valentinrussanov (1); ©m-imagephotography (5); ©yopinco (5, 84, 139, 148); ©LightFieldStudios (84); ©ajijchan (139); ©drbimages (148); **Shutterstock:** ©yopinco (avatar bodies 5, 6, 8, 9, 10, 11, 16, 28, 32, 34, 36, 38, 40, 47, 56, 63, 65, 70, 77, 80, 84, 93, 95, 101, 103, 108, 116, 120, 126, 136, 139, 148, 150, 152); ©Alona Rieznichek (7); ©Alice Vacca (8 CTR RT); ©dedMazay (8 LO LE); ©Farah Sadikhova (9 LO RT, 11 LO LE); ©helion19 (9 CTR LE); ©lineartestpilot (9 UP RT, 113); ©Antonov Maxim (10 UP RT); ©Katrinshine (10 CTR); ©wenchiawang (10 LO RT); ©kostolom3000 (11 UP RT); ©LightField Studios (12); ©Olesia Bilkei (13); ©Andre Helbig (14 CTR LE); ©ajt (14 LO LE); ©DVBecker (14 UP CTR); ©Eaks1979 (14 LO CTR); ©endeavor (14 CTR RT); ©horiyan (14 LO RT); ©Hurst Photo (14 UP RT); ©Tapui (14 UP CTR); ©andregric (15 LO CTR); ©anmbph (15 CTR RT); ©Bernd Schmidt (15 LO RT); ©Kitch Bain (15 CTR1 LE); ©little birdie (15 CTR2 LE); ©Lovely Bird (15 LO LE); ©margouillat photo (15 UP CTR); ©Purple Moon (15 CTR2); ©Richard Peterson (15 CTR1); ©Tobik (15 UP LE); ©urfin (15 UP RT); ©12 Studio (16 UP CTR); ©Anton Starikov (16 LO CTR); ©bogdan ionescu (16 LO LE); ©GS Creations (16 UP LE); ©Shubhere (16 LO RT, 25 CTR LE); ©Studio KIWI (16 UP RT); ©Trong Nguyen (16 CTR RT); ©Christopher Hall (40); ©Silver Kitten+G183 (68); ©Cory Thoman (83); ©Alongkorn Sanguansook (85); ©START-ART (128, 129); ©Mi_daria (131 UP LE)

Cover and book design by Tandem Books

Library of Congress Cataloging-in-Publication Data
Available on request

10 9 8 7 6 5 4 3 2 1

Published by Hearst Home Kids, an imprint of
Hearst Books/Hearst Communications, Inc.
300 W 57th Street
New York, NY 10019

For information about custom editions, special sales, premium and corporate purchases: hearst.com/magazines/hearst-books

Printed in Canada

ISBN 978-1-950785-62-9